PIANO MUSIC OF
LOUIS MOREAU
Gottschalk

PIANO MUSIC OF
LOUIS MOREAU
Gottschalk

26 Complete Pieces from Original Editions

SELECTED AND INTRODUCED BY

Richard Jackson
Head, Americana Collection,
Library and Museum of the Performing Arts,
New York Public Library

DOVER PUBLICATIONS, INC.
NEW YORK

ACKNOWLEDGEMENTS

The publisher would like to thank Mr. William Lloyd Keepers for making this collection possible by lending the bulk of the sheet music reproduced. Gratitude is also expressed to The New York Public Library and the Eastman School of Music for their generous loans of sheet music.

Copyright © 1973 by Dover Publications, Inc.
All rights reserved under Pan American and International Copyright Conventions.

Published in Canada by General Publishing Company, Ltd., 30 Lesmill Road, Don Mills, Toronto, Ontario.
Published in the United Kingdom by Constable and Company, Ltd., 10 Orange Street, London WC 2.

Piano Music of Louis Moreau Gottschalk: 26 Complete Pieces from Original Editions is a new collection of music, selected and introduced by Richard Jackson and first published by Dover Publications, Inc. in 1973. The original publishers and dates of publication of the music appear on the individual title pages.

International Standard Book Number: 0–486–21683–7
Library of Congress Catalog Card Number: 73–75872

Manufactured in the United States of America
Dover Publications, Inc.
180 Varick Street
New York, N.Y. 10014

Gottschalk of Louisiana

Speaking in Warsaw in October 1972 during a tour of the New York City Ballet, George Balanchine told reporters that he was glad his company had the opportunity of appearing before foreign audiences: "Europeans feel that we [Americans] can only build machines and automobiles. They think we have no soul." [1]

If Balanchine's assessment was credible in 1972, one can only imagine the degree of reluctance of the European cultural establishment to accept an American musician in the middle of the nineteenth century. Louis Moreau Gottschalk, fresh from New Orleans at age thirteen, was among the first American musicians to be confronted with this attitude when he sought entrance to the Paris Conservatoire in 1842. He was rejected by Pierre Zimmermann, director of piano classes, without an audition. Curiously enough, the essence of the rejection (as mentioned twice by Gottschalk in his diary years later) is similar to that of Balanchine's comment: Zimmermann had advised him that the Conservatoire was no place for an American, since his country "was only a land of steam engines" ". . . the country of railroads but not of musicians." [2]

Gottschalk, of course, easily triumphed over such prejudice during his ten-year residence in Europe, first as a brilliant student and subsequently as a piano virtuoso and composer lionized in the salons and concert halls, "fondled and fêted everywhere," [3] as one journalist in Geneva put it. It might be said that Gottschalk's nationality actually proved to be something of an asset in his early career. One aspect of the Romantic aesthetic was a fascination with the exotic and faraway, and as American, Gottschalk and his music were exotic to Europeans largely ignorant about the country. (Gottschalk recalled in his diary a conversation with the Grand Duchess of Russia who was under the impression that P. T. Barnum was a prominent American statesman!) In 1848 a writer in *La France Musicale* was exclaiming: "We have discovered this Creole composer; an American composer, *bon Dieu*!" and describing his music as "wild, languishing, indescribable, which has no resemblance to any other European music." [4]

By 1851 Hector Berlioz, for some time one of Gottschalk's most important supporters, was writing: "Mr. Gottschalk was born in America, whence he has brought a host of curious chants from the Creoles and Negroes; he has made from them the themes of his most delicious compositions. Everybody in Europe now knows *Bamboula*, *Le Bananier*, *Le Mancenillier*, *La Savane*, and twenty other ingenious fantasies in which the nonchalant graces of tropical melody assuage so agreeably our restless and insatiable passion for novelty." [5]

That same year Théophile Gautier was placing Gottschalk's music among other celebrated exotic products: ". . . we have also been as much charmed by the melodious strains of the American artist, as we already have been by the chants of the muezzin, and the reveries under the palms which Félicien David and Ernest Reyer have noted with their souvenirs of the east."[6]

Youthful geniuses were hardly an unknown breed in European music circles, but a youthful *American* genius was a strange apparition indeed. It is certainly not an insignificant detail that in Gottschalk's earliest published music in France his name appears with the accompanying phrase "de la Louisiane." It was a fact too remarkable for the publisher to let pass.

When Gottschalk returned to America in January 1853 to launch his domestic career, the fact of his native birth was no longer a remarkable consideration in itself or capable of stirring unusual curiosity. It was the glow of Gottschalk's advance European reputation—reports had circulated in the American press for years—which aroused the interest of his concert-going countrymen.

Gottschalk had the distinction of being the first American concert artist to gain international fame prior to a career in this country. It was, unfortunately, a pattern which became a curse to succeeding generations of native artists. Here was a variation on the phenomenon at least as old as the New Testament: it was not that Americans would not honor native prophets in their own land; rather that they would honor them after the sanctification of European training or critical acclaim or, ideally, both.

From Gottschalk's day well into the twentieth century, scores of young composers and performers trooped to the cultural capitals of the Old World (Germany, most popular at first; France, fashionable later on) for training and experience. They returned certified, with diaries full of Clara Schumann, Liszt, Rheinberger, Widor—and later—d'Indy, Stravinsky and Nadia Boulanger. The European mystique persists even in the last quarter of the twentieth century: it is not uncommon for singers and other performers to throw away their "Smiths" and "Blacks" to become "Schmidt-Hausers" and "Schwarzbergs," believing, with some justification, that a European name will give them an advantage, even without European credentials.

Gottschalk's American career was not accompanied by a unanimous chorus of critical approbation. He received hundreds of good notices and the support of such important musicians as Richard Hoffman and William Mason, but he also received a number of bad notices, especially in New England where John S. Dwight, the influential journalist, and others criticized him as a superficial showman. His career was marked, however, with consistent and overwhelming popular success. He was one of the most adored artists of his day, rivaled perhaps only by Jenny Lind. And despite his seriousness and sophistication as a composer and performer, it is as the popular figure par excellence that he should no doubt be best remembered. If Gottschalk were transposed to a later day, he might be regarded as a combination of Fritz Kreisler, the great artist tossing out delicious compositional bonbons, Kurt Weill, the profound composer speaking naturally in the popular style, and Virgil Fox, the theatrical virtuoso performer sweeping back his cape to take a bow.

In America the "irresistible prestige"[7] (as Berlioz had put it) which seemed to surround Gottschalk was due only in part to his glamorous European reputation. Not only was his playing magical, but he exerted a peculiar hold over his audiences by his manner and style, by his personality and physical appearance. Over and over again contemporary accounts attest to his appeal:

—From the diary of an eye-witness of his first New York concerts: "He is very young looking, does not seem to be over twenty-two years of age, handsome, and, to crown the whole, is so easy and unaffected in his manner that a person could not fail to be pleased with him as a man."[8]

—From a review of his first New Orleans concert after returning from Europe: "A small, pale, delicate looking young man—almost a boy in form and appearance—of chestnut hair, large dreamy blue eyes, a pleasant well shaped countenance and modest demeanor, stood bowing before this audience that received him in the heartiest and most encouraging manner. . . . To brilliancy and vigor . . . he unites a delicacy, a finish, an ease and above all a poetical grace and feeling that are peculiarly his own."[9]

—From Richard Hoffman: " . . . after a few moments the fire would kindle and he would play with all the brilliancy which was so peculiarly his own. He was possessed of a ringing, scintillating touch, which, joined to a poetic charm of expression, seemed to sway the emotions of his audience with almost hypnotic power. His eyes were the striking feature of his face, large and dark with peculiarly drooping lids, which always appeared half closed as he played."[10]

Hoffman also gave us a description of Gottschalk's inimitable platform manner: "It was the fashion at that time always to wear white gloves with evening dress, and his manner of taking them off, after seating himself at the piano, was often a very amusing episode. His deliberation, his perfect indifference to the waiting audience was thoroughly manifest, as he slowly drew them off one finger at a time, bowing and smiling meanwhile to the familiar faces in the front rows. Finally disposing of them, he would manipulate his hands until they were quite limber, then preludize until his mood prompted him to begin his selection on the programme."[11]

A measure of the adoration Gottschalk elicited is suggested by a remark of the pianist Amy Fay in a letter from Germany while she was a student; in early 1870, after hearing of Gottschalk's death, she wrote: "I was dreadfully sorry to hear of poor Gottschalk's death. He had a golden touch, and equal to any in the world, I think. . . . If anything more is in the papers about him you must send it to me, for the infatuation that I and 999,999 other American girls once felt for him, still lingers in my breast!"[12] It is apt that Gottschalk has been called America's first matinee idol.[13]

Pleasing the public was apparently one of his strongest motivations as an artist. While he did perform works of Mozart, Beethoven, Chopin and Weber, among others, his programs consisted largely of his own popular compositions, from the glittering fantasies on favorite opera melodies to the infectious Negro and Caribbean dance pieces, and always *The Last Hope*, with women swooning or rushing to the stage to snatch a souvenir. The celebrated pianist Teresa Carreño, at one time a pupil of Gottschalk, is quoted as saying that he "thought himself capable of much better than he published; and he said that when the public was ready to advance he would be found in the vanguard."[14] The remarkable fact is that he *was*, in a real sense, "in the vanguard" beginning with early compositions such as *Bamboula*. This piece, still astonishing in its modernity, *The Banjo, Souvenir de Porto Rico*, and many others so popular with his audiences everywhere, were daring and original conceptions at the time. Nothing like them had been heard before and nothing like them would be heard for decades to come. Throughout his career he continued to please audiences with original material, much of it of considerable artistry and stature.

Gottschalk was not only an artist of great popularity; he was the country's first "popularizer" of concert music on a grand scale. He gave hundreds of recitals all over the country, not only in the larger cities but in small towns and villages. He travelled more than any other major concert pianist of his day. His diary is filled with details of these travels—the uncomfortable railway cars, stifling in summer, cold and drafty in winter; the sickening ordeal of stagecoach travel; the occasionally indifferent audiences, half-empty houses, and meager box-office receipts. Gottschalk played in frontier mining towns and on the edge of Civil War battlefields, where he operated a kind of high-class U.S.O. show. It would be impossible to estimate the number of Americans whose first exposure to professional concert music-making was due to the indefatigable Louis Moreau.

After Gottschalk's return from Europe in 1853, he was to live for only sixteen years. He never returned to the scenes of his first triumphs, though he did leave the country for extensive tours in the West Indies and South America. He conducted gigantic concerts in Cuba and elsewhere employing hundreds of performers. Massive musical shows of this kind had been staged by Berlioz in France, and his friend Gottschalk decided to try his hand at them in the New World. They invariably left audiences gasping and the maestro in a state of collapse.

There were periods of languorous inactivity in the tropics and periods of feverish composition: dozens of piano pieces, vocal works, two symphonies, and works for piano and orchestra flew from his pen. Many pieces which Gottschalk performed in the tropics and elsewhere were never written down; others were notated but never published, including a fascinating little collection of exercises and technical studies for the piano on which Gottschalk collaborated with N. R. Espadero, a Cuban pianist and disciple.

He never married, preferring rather the life of gypsy-musician-adventurer. He acquired a notorious reputation for his sexual exploits and fathered at least one child. At his death in Rio de Janeiro on December 18, 1869 at age forty, he was a man exhausted both physically and emotionally. He was also nearly broke. Though he earned a considerable fortune over the years, it was spent largely on others: the long-distance support of his mother who had followed him to Paris in 1847 and who died there in 1856; the liquidation of debts left by his father upon his death in New Orleans in 1853; a pension for his childhood slave-nurse Sally; innumerable gifts and handouts to friends and anyone else in need who appealed to his sympathies. His generosity became proverbial, just as his name has become synonymous with all that was brilliant, poetic and original in American piano music of the mid-nineteenth century.

NOTES ON THE MUSIC

(The "RO" numbers cited with titles here refer to Robert Offergeld's definitive list of Gottschalk's compositions published as *The Centennial Catalogue of the Published and Unpublished Compositions of Louis Moreau Gottschalk* (New York: Ziff-Davis Publishing Co., 1970). The dates of compositions given here were established by Offergeld.)

I. United States Ethnic and Patriotic Music

The man who was America's first internationalist in music was also its first nationalist. When Gottschalk began composing music while a teenager in France, he quite spontaneously used native goods from home as his raw material. It has been suggested that three of the famous early pieces, *Bamboula*, *Le Bananier*, and *La Savane*, could be called his Louisiana trilogy.[15] I would add *Le Mancenillier*, making it a quartet, and call it Gottschalk's "Scenes from My Childhood."

Bamboula, Danse de Nègres (RO 20; 1844–45) utilizes a Creole folk melody identified with the text *Quand patate la cuite na va mangé li*! ("When that 'tater's cooked don't you eat it up!"). The song was used in New Orleans with a Negro dance called the bamboula derived from a drum of the same name. During Gottschalk's childhood, the bamboula could be seen and heard in Congo Square, a weekend gathering place for Negroes. Whether the young Moreau was actually taken to the Square by his slave-nurse is not known; it is certain, however, that the singing and drumming could be heard from the balcony of the family home scarcely two blocks from the Square on North Rampart Street.

The fantastic spectacle of the bamboula was described years later by George W. Cable in his article "The Dance in Place Congo" (1886). He speaks of the "booming of African drums and blast of huge wooden horns," the use of triangles, Jew's harps, rattles, banjo, and the slap of bare feet on earth.[16] Gottschalk's *Bamboula* distills the savagery of the original and yet is marvelously evocative: the pounding octaves, the syncopated banjo figures, the tension and surprise. It is one of the remarkable piano pieces of the nineteenth century.

When New Orleans heard Gottschalk perform the piece for the first time in 1853, it marked not only the homecoming of a native celebrity but also the return of a bit of local melody after a sea-change: "The 'Bamboula' was received literally with a whirlwind of the most vehement expressions of admirations; magnificent bouquets fell by twenties on the platform. . . . Every one had been waiting for this piece and every one was delighted with it."[17]

Le Bananier, Chanson Nègre (RO 21; *ca.* 1845–46) derives from the Creole song "En avan' Grenadie." It is a beguiling piece, beginning with a suggestion of drumming, proceeding with several repetitions of the melody (in minor and major) surrounded by changing figurations, to a brilliant finish. It was one of Gottschalk's first great successes; it was taken up by numerous pianists (including Alfred Jaell who played it in New York prior to Gottschalk's return), went through many European and American printings, and was transcribed for the cello by Offenbach.

The Banjo, Grotesque Fantasie, American Sketch (RO 22; *ca.* 1854–55) is Gottschalk in a front-row seat at the minstrel show. The theatrical cover design of the Hall edition reprinted in this collection veritably invites us to come in. It is the composer at his smiling-American best. *The Banjo* is the kind of crackling good commercial showpiece which Gottschalk pulled off so well, though perhaps never again quite so well as here. Just as the piece seems on the verge of becoming too repetitious, a tune very close to Stephen Foster's "Camptown Races" emerges and we're off to a *prestissimo* finish which sounds like a virtuoso banjo-picker on a particularly good day.

In *La Savane, Ballade Créole* (RO 232; *ca.* 1845–46), Gottschalk again used the melody of a folk song remembered from New Orleans. The song is known as "Lolotte" or "Pov' piti Lolotte" and can be found in several folksong collections. The title of Gottschalk's piece could refer to the kind of landscape which was familiar to him as a child. Looking northeast from the balcony of the North Rampart Street house, he could view the swampy savanna with its growths of palmetto and moss-draped cypress trees stretching toward Lake Pontchartrain.

The piece which Gottschalk fashioned from the familiar tune is deft, simple and haunting. After a twenty-measure introduction—recitative-like, based on a fragment of the tune—the construction of the piece is similar to *Le Bananier*: repeated statements of the tune with changing accompaniments and figurations.

In 1862 Gottschalk made his musical contribution to the war effort with *Union, Paraphrase de Concert* (RO 269), which he dedicated to Gen. George McClellan. Despite his background and fondness for things southern (especially New Orleans), Gottschalk was a unionist and an abolitionist. He performed the piece all over the North and East during the war for soldiers and civilians alike. In 1864 President and Mrs. Lincoln heard Gottschalk play *Union*; in 1865 the composer once again played the piece for Lincoln, this time as part of a shipboard memorial service organized en route to California after news of the assassination was received.

It is a combination of *The Star Spangled Banner*, *Hail Columbia* and *Yankee Doodle* interspersed with thunderous octave passages and imitations of drums, cannons and bugles.

II. Music from Spain

Crowning Gottschalk's European career was his eighteen-month tour of Spain in 1851–52, after which he returned briefly to Paris and then embarked for America in December of the latter year. He made a great hit in Spain; he entertained constantly, and was himself entertained, at the Court and was decorated by Queen Isabella II. He played all over the provinces and at big public events. Predictably, the music dating from the visit, or written later upon reflection, contains native Spanish elements: quotations from traditional tunes or original tunes in traditional style and several dance forms and rhythms.

Gottschalk tells us (in French) on the title page of the published score that *La Jota Aragonesa, Caprice Espagnol* (RO 130; 1852) is a fragment of the "Grande Symphonie for 10 pianos, 'El Sitio de Zaragoza' performed in Madrid on 28 June 1852 . . ." This Grande Symphonie was probably the composer's first foray into the monster-concert business. (The score of the Symphonie did not survive.) The jota is a Spanish dance, and Gottschalk's brilliant version is modeled on the dance as found in Aragon. The jota by Massenet (his famous *Aragonaise*), composed in 1885 for the ballet in his opera *Le Cid*, is quite reminiscent of Gottschalk's 1852 treatment.

Manchega, Etude de Concert (RO 143) was possibly conceived during the Spanish sojourn. The score is dated "Seville 1853–1860," which makes no literal sense. Could it be that Gottschalk performed the piece in Seville but further shaped it and wrote it down in finished form between 1853 and 1860 (the copyright date)? In any case, it is a real etude—a fast, difficult study in repeated figures and cross-rhythms demanding total independence of the hands. It also calls to mind the sounds of a Mexican mariachi band.

Minuit à Séville, Caprice (RO 170). One catalogue gives 1852 for this work and another 1856, so it may be that, like *Manchega*, it was conceived in Spain and notated later on. Certainly there is no mistaking the Spanish qualities of the piece. It abounds in typical guitar figures, flamenco rhythm, and a suggestion of castanets. Gottschalk begins with eleven measures of scene painting (there are twelve *fortissimo* octaves and chords along the way—it is midnight indeed) before digging into his guitar-strumming reverie. He also quotes a traditional Andalusian verse as a head note for the piece; here is a rough translation:

> In the midst of my troubles
> I wanted to go to sleep,
> For one who lives like me
> When he sleeps, he lives.

Souvenirs d'Andalousie, Caprice de Concert (RO 242; 1851). A note on the cover of the score indicates (in part) that this piece was improvised at a concert in Madrid on 16 December 1851. It uses three traditional dance patterns and tunes—the fandango, cana and jaleo de Jerez. The most famous theme is the fandango which was also used by Glinka in his *Capriccio Brillante on the Jota Aragonesa* (1845) and in modern times by Ernesto Lecuona as the basis for his *Malagueña*.

III. West Indian Souvenirs

Gottschalk first visited Cuba in 1853 and 1854. He was to return several times between 1857 and 1862, occasionally remaining for extended periods; during this time he also toured Puerto Rico, Haiti, and other islands. Just as he was alert to the possibilities of using folk and popular materials of Spain and the United States in his compositions, so it was during his travels in the West Indies. He found the tango rhythms and insinuating melodic patterns of tropical music irresistible and quite suited to his temperament. Furthermore, he was shrewd enough and experienced enough to know what effect the use of familiar materials had upon local audiences.

Danza (RO 66) is dated "Porto-Rico Novembre 1857." It begins with an elegant French-style polka, but at measure eighteen swings into a typical Puerto Rican *danza* with habanera rhythm—a combination which could be called typically "Gottschalkian." The composer was obviously fond of this piece; he used it as the basis of his *Escenas Campestres* (1860), a *scena* (or one-act opera, as he called it) for soprano, tenor, baritone, and orchestra, set to verses by a Cuban poet.

La Gallina (*The Hen*), *Danse Cubaine* (RO 101; *ca.* 1859) is a very funny descriptive piece. Gottschalk's Cuban chicken struts to the habanera rhythm but also at times seems on the verge of a cakewalk. At the last page, with its curious unresolved seventh chords, we have a kind of mid-nineteenth-century jazz—the squawking, syncopated left hand working against the relentless, mechanical-piano right hand.

Though *Le Mancenillier, Sérénade* (RO 142) appears in certain editions with the subtitle *West Indian Serenade*, and thus belongs in the Caribbean group, it was probably composed in 1849, years before Gottschalk saw the Indies. It was one of the very popular pieces of Gottschalk's European years. Perhaps it would be more accurate to place it alongside the early pieces inspired by childhood musical recollections, for it is conceivable that the melody is an echo of West Indian songs heard in his maternal grandparents' home. The Bruslés had immigrated from Haiti via Jamaica to New Orleans as a result of the Haitian revolution of the 1790's.

Certainly it is clear that Gottschalk's French reviewers understood the piece to be similar in origin to *La Savane* and the others. Adolphe Adam, remembered for his ballet *Giselle* and the Christmas song *Cantique de Noël*, wrote in 1850: "The memories of childhood recalled to him the negro [sic] airs to which he had been nursed; he translated them upon his keyboard, and we have the 'Bananier,' the 'Bamboula,' 'Manceniller,' [sic] and those charming and simple melodies which art and science extract in the most distinguished way."[18]

O, Ma Charmante, Épargnez Moi! (*O My Charmer, Spare Me*), *Caprice* (RO 182; 1861). Gottschalk obviously took great care with this work. It is a succinct, well-crafted and most expressive piece. If one can believe the implications of the title, the work may have had a programmatic background. Gottschalk's long technical note in French and English printed in the score is an indication of his desire that the performer take as much care in executing the piece as he did in composing it. The second note, in English (written by the publisher or perhaps Gottschalk himself), assures us that the *morceau* is entirely original and instructs us that as Chopin "transfered the national traits of Poland, to his Mazurkas and Polonaises . . . Gottschalk has endeavored to reproduce in works of an appropriate character, the characteristic traits of the Dances of the West Indias."

Ojos Criollos (*Les Yeux Créoles*), *Danse Cubaine, Caprice Brillant* (RO 185; 1859) is reprinted here in its solo version. On the cover of the four-hand version is a note in French which says: "Performed by the composer and Mr. Espadero of Havana with great success and requested at all their concerts." And no wonder. It is one of Gottschalk's most scintillating polka-tango transformations. Creole eyes obviously had a salubrious effect on the composer.

Among Gottschalk's memorable "souvenirs" of the West Indies are his *Souvenir de Porto Rico, Marche des Gibaros* (RO 250; 1857) and *Souvenir de la Havane, Grande Caprice de Concert* (RO 246; 1859). Both are large, ambitious pieces full of characteristic syncopation and sensuous tunes. The Puerto Rican piece is the more famous of the two and more successful on its own terms. The Havana caprice is weakened by a certain monotony, for all its considerable charm. *Souvenir de Porto Rico* is a "patrol" march in that it is based on the repetition of material, beginning softly, building to a big climax, and receding into the sunset. Its cross-rhythms are original and difficult. (Incidently, *gibaros* are Puerto Rican peasants, and the tune used by Gottschalk is an authentic folk song.)

Suis Moi! Caprice (RO 253; ca. 1861) is all *brillante, con eleganza, con bravura,* and three-against-two. The lengthy note by Gottschalk on the technique of performing Creole music, which appeared in *O, Ma Charmante,* was again used here.

IV. Concert and Salon Music (Non-nationalistic)

Gottschalk of course composed many works which were not specifically nationalistic or folkloristic in character. Among these were several popular favorites of recital audiences and amateur pianists. In fact, two or three of the salon pieces became so entrenched they came, wrongly, to constitute Gottschalk's entire reputation as a composer before the revival of interest in his music began in the 1930's and 1940's.

Sixième Ballade (RO 14; date of composition unknown) is a very American ballade—simple, direct, sentimental. Gottschalk composed eight ballades (the best of them were not so called, however, in published form), but he did not seem particularly at home in this form. When it came to the salon *genre*, with such pieces as *Berceuse, Cradle Song* (RO 27; 1860) and *The Dying Poet, Meditation* (RO 75; *ca.* 1863–64), Gottschalk was indeed at home. He was tremendously adept at catching that "pathetic" quality so dear to Victorian audiences. For the salon pieces, he fashioned simple but memorable tunes and placed them in settings that were sonorous and a bit tricky, though not so tricky that they could not be mastered by the talented amateur. (Gottschalk eventually played a number of these pieces in his recitals, but on the published music he would occasionally use a pseudonym; "Seven Octaves" and "Oscar Litti" were two.)

Both *Berceuse* and *The Dying Poet* have a share of filigree traceries high in the treble which sound more difficult than they are to play. *Berceuse* has crossing hands and *The Dying Poet* furious repeated octaves, all of which are particularly effective in the parlor.

The Last Hope, Religious Meditation (RO 133; 1854) is Gottschalk's most famous salon piece and, for decades, the one work most closely associated with his name. Since its appearance well over a century ago, it has, quite literally, always been with us. At no time has it been totally unavailable in some form, whether in published sheet music or collections, cylinders, piano rolls, records or music boxes. Many Protestant churches in America and elsewhere have harbored it since 1888, when Rev. Edwin Pond Parker, a Congregational minister in Hartford, Connecticut, transformed Gottschalk's slow "religioso" waltz into the hymn tune *Mercy*. In this guise it has been used with the texts "Holy Ghost, with Light Divine," "Father of Eternal Grace" and several others.

Gottschalk composed *The Last Hope* in Cuba in 1854 and refers to it in his diary; he mentions composing a few pieces at the time, "one of them of a melancholy character with which was connected a touching episode of my journey to Santiago, Cuba, that seemed to me to unite the conditions requisite for popularity."[19] How right he was!

Morte!! (*She Is Dead*), *Lamentation* (RO 174; probably 1868) was Gottschalk's last big celebration of tragedy in the parlor. It was very popular in South America during his last months. When he sent the manuscript to his publisher in October 1869, he wrote: "I believe it to be my best effort for years. [Was he being the salesman here?] Ever since I have played it it has been encored, and a great many women have hysterics and weep over it."[20] What more could any composer want? *Morte!!* also became an object of morbid fascination in this country because of the long-lasting (but apocryphal) story that the composer actually fell dead at the keyboard while playing the piece in his last concert in Rio. (He was carried out ill from the concert and died several days later.)

The four remaining works in this collection are far removed from religious meditations, dying poets, and lamentations over dead girls. *Grand Scherzo* (RO 114; 1869), another late work, is indeed grand and superbly pianistic. If there is a temptation to regard the piece as merely Chopinesque, examine the middle section (*Un poco meno mosso*): it could only have been written by an American remembering the songs of home.

Pasquinade, Caprice (RO 189; *ca.* 1869) and *Ses Yeux, Polka de Concert* (RO 235; 1865) are two of Gottschalk's happiest creations. The former is surely a gavotte, but its second strain (measure 21) introduces the lightly syncopated treble figures over the steady bass which two decades later would emerge as the key feature of the cakewalk, with ragtime hard on its heels. *Ses Yeux* could have been a celebration to end the Civil War. It is dashing and relentlessly optimistic, despite the spice of an occasional passing dissonance.

Gottschalk's *Tournament Galop* (RO 264; probably 1854), "played by him at all his concerts throughout the United States," says the publisher's blurb, is all fanfares, drums, high spirits. It is the composer out-of-doors, without a hat on, enjoying some great American show—but with chilled French champagne close at hand, to be sure.

RICHARD JACKSON

New York, November 1972

NOTES

1. *The New York Times*, October 23, 1972.
2. Louis Moreau Gottschalk, *Notes of a Pianist* (New York: Alfred A. Knopf, 1964), pp. 52, 221.
3. Quoted in W. S. B. Mathews, "Gottschalk—A Successful American Composer," *Music* II (June 1892), p. 121.
4. *Ibid.*, p. 119.
5. *Feuilleton du Journal des Débats*, Paris, April 13, 1851.
6. Quoted in Mathews, *Music*, p. 124.
7. *Ibid.*, p. 122.
8. *Ibid.*, p. 124.
9. New Orleans *Daily Picayune*, April 7, 1853.
10. *Some Musical Recollections of Fifty Years* (New York: Charles Scribner's Sons, 1910), p. 135.
11. *Ibid.*, pp. 133–34.
12. *Music-Study in Germany* (New York: The Macmillan Company, 1897; Dover Publications, 1965), p. 42.
13. The title of a chapter in Irving Lowens, *Music and Musicians in Early America* (New York: W. W. Norton & Co., Inc., 1964).
14. Quoted in W. S. B. Mathews, "L. M. Gottschalk, The Most Popular of American Composers," *The Musician* XIII/10 (October 1908), p. 440.
15. Gilbert Chase, *America's Music* (New York: McGraw-Hill Book Company, 1966), p. 315.
16. Quoted in *Ibid.*, p. 307.
17. New Orleans *Daily Picayune*, April 14, 1853.
18. Quoted in Mathews, *Music*, p. 123.
19. *Notes of a Pianist*, pp. 48–49.
20. Quoted in William Arms Fisher, "Louis Moreau Gottschalk, The First American Pianist and Composer; A Life Sketch," *The Musician* XIII/10 (October 1908), p. 438.

Contents

IV. Concert and Salon Music (Non-nationalistic)

United States Ethnic and Patriotic Music

à sa Majesté

ISABELLE II
Reine des Espagnes

BAMBOULA

Danse des Negres.

𝕱𝖆𝖓𝖙𝖆𝖎𝖘𝖎𝖊

POUR

PIANO

PAR

L. M. GOTTSCHALK.

de la Louisiane.

Op: 2.

Propriété des Editeurs Enregistré aux Archives de l'Union

Pr. 1 fl. 30 kr.

MAYENCE
ANVERS ET BRUXELLES
chez les fils de B. Schott

Dépôt général de notre fonds de Musique. a Leipzig, chez C. F. Leede. à Vienne, chez H. F. Müller

à Londres, chez Schott et Cie 89, St James's Street

10301

BAMBOULA

DANSE DE NEGRES.

L. M. GOTTSCHALK Op: 2.

de la Louisiane.

LE

BANANIER.

CHANSON NÉGRE.

EXECUTÉ PAR MESSIEURS

JAELL

ET

GOTTSCHALK

Composée par

L.M. GOTTSCHALK.

BOSTON.

Published by **OLIVER DITSON** 115 Washington St.

25 ¢ net

| J.E.GOULD & Cº | T.T. BARKER | D.A. TRUAX | C.C. CLAPP & Cº | T.S: BERRY & Cº |
| Philª | Boston | Cincinnati | Boston. | N.York. |

Greene Eng

LE BANANIER.

To
Richard Hoffman.

GROTESQUE FANTASIE

THE

BANJO

AN AMERICAN SKETCH

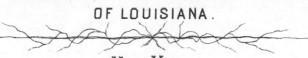

COMPOSED BY

L. M. Gottschalk.

OF LOUISIANA.

J.C.Pearson, N.Y.

☆ 10

New York

Published by WILLIAM HALL & SON, 239 Broadway.

Paris, BUREAU CENTRAL.   Madrid, MARTIN.   Mayence, SCHOTT FILS.
Londres, SCHOTT FRÉRES.   Milan, LUCCA.   Lisbon, NEUMAN.

Entered according to Act of Congress AD 1855 by Wm. Hall & Son, in the Clerk's Office of the District Court of the Southern District of New York.

Printed by J.H.Colton & Co.

"THE BANJO"

BY

GOTTSCHALK.

Facilité.

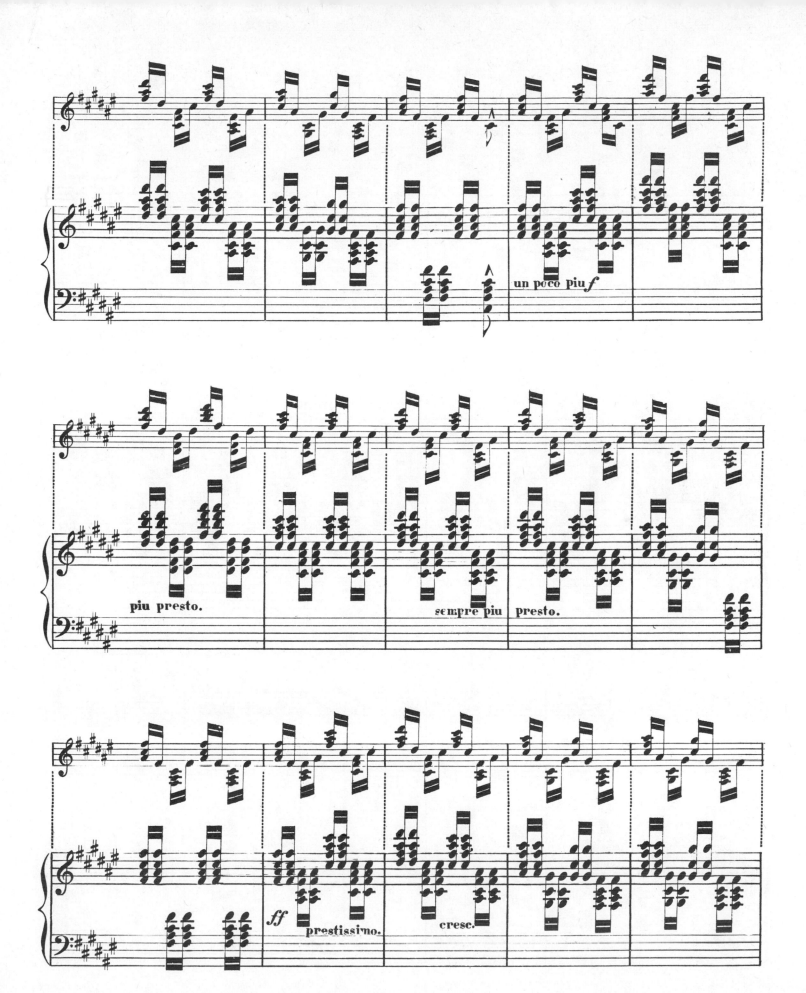

Clayton, Eng.ᵛᵉ

LA SAVANE

Ballade Créole

pour le Piano

Composée par

L. M. GOTTSCHALK.

de la Louisiane.

Op. 3. — 50 *ᵏ* net.

PHILADELPHIA.
Published by J. E. GOULD & Cᵒ 126 Chesnut Stᵗ
Successors of A. FIOT.

Boston. OLIVER DITSON.   N. York, T. S. BERRY & Cᵒ   Boston, C. C. CLAPP & Cᵒ

2190   Greene Eng

LA SAVANE.

BALLADE CREOLE

L. M. GOTTSCHALK. Op: 3.

de la Louisiane.

TO

Majr. Genl. Geo. B. McClellan.

UNION

Paraphrase de Concert.

on the National airs

STAR SPANGLED BANNER, YANKEE DOODLE, & HAIL COLUMBIA.

Composed by

L. M. GOTTSCHALK.

15

NEW YORK
Published by Wm. HALL & SON 543 Broadway.
Boston O. DITSON & CO.   ROOT & CADY Chicago.

"UNION"

PARAPHRASE DE CONCERT.

L. M. GOTTSCHALK.

"THE STAR-SPANGLED BANNER."

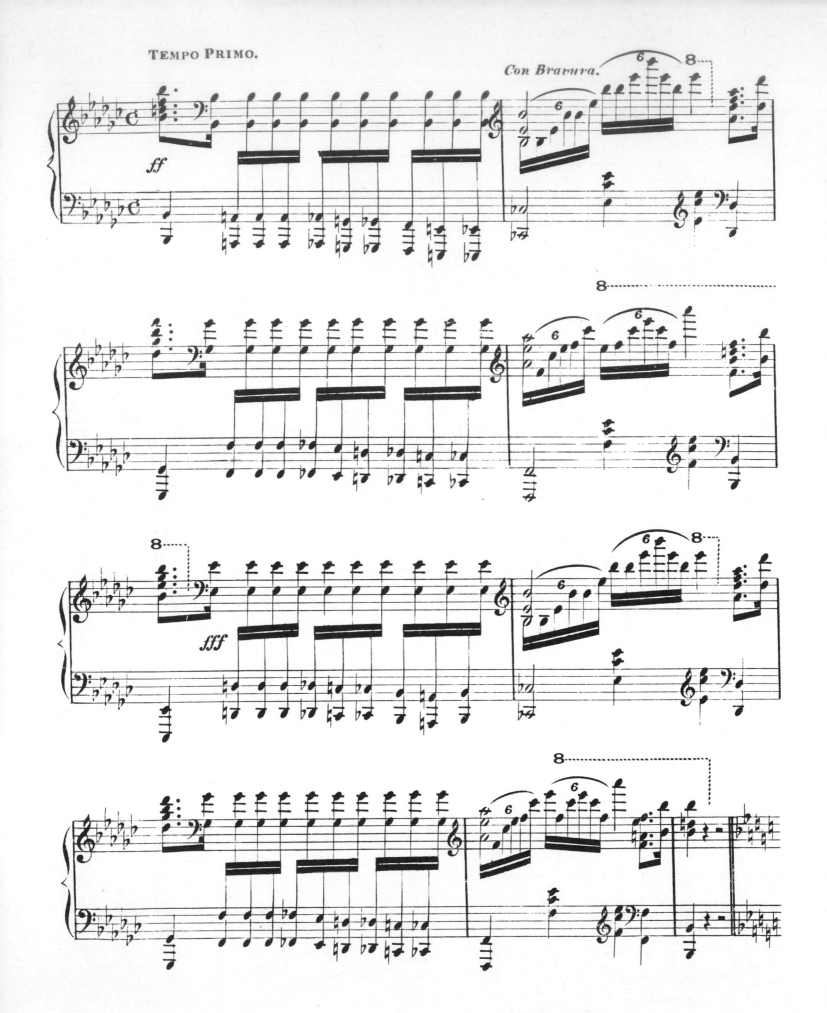

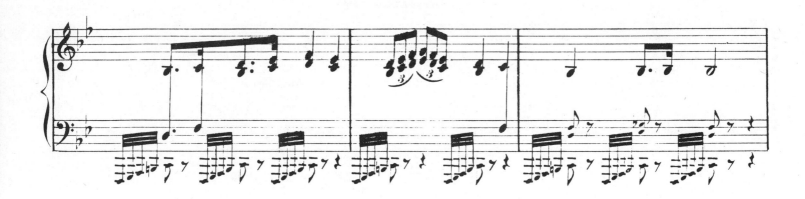

Allontanandosi.

Perpendosi.

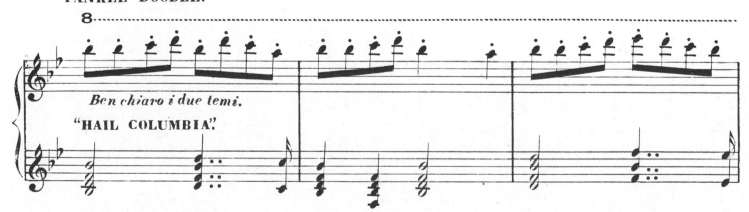

"YANKEE DOODLE."

Ben chiaro i due temi.

"HAIL COLUMBIA."

Clayton.

Music from Spain

A MON  "MI"

Monsieur Letellier,

Témoignage d'affection et de reconnaissance.

LA JOTA ARAGONESA

CAPRICE ESPAGNOL

Composé par

L. M. GOTTSCHALK.

Tire de la grande symphonie à 10 Pianos "EL SITIO DE ZARAGOZA" exécutée à Madrid, le 28 Juin 1852, devant toute la Cour d'Espagne, et qui valut à son auteur le titre de Chevalier, la croix en brillants d'Isabelle la Catholique et l'épée d'honneur qui lui fut présentée par "El Chiclanero".

NEW YORK

Published by **WILLIAM HALL & SON**, 239 Broadway.

PARIS.   „ BUREAU CENTRAL.

MAYENCE.   „ SCHOTT & FILS.

LONDON.   „ SCHOTT.

MILAN.   „ LUCCA.

TEMOIGNAGE D'AFFECTION ET DE RECONNAISSANCE.

a
mon vieux maître et ami
Mr LETELLIER.

LA JOTA ARAGONESA

CAPRICE ESPAGNOL
Composé pour le
PIANO
par
L. M. GOTTSCHALK.

(tivé de la grande symphonie
à 10 Pianos
"EL SITIO DE ZARAGOZA")

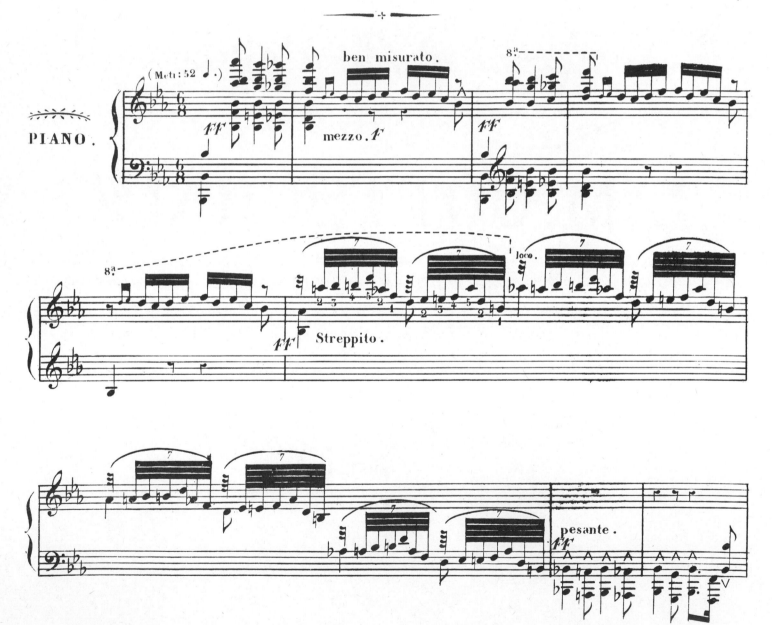

MANCHECA

Etude de Concert

COMPOSEE PAR

L. M. Gottschalk.

W.H. LEESON.

NEW YORK

Published by Wm HALL & SON. 543 Broadway.

London.	Paris.	Mayence.	Madrid.	Lisbon.
SCHOTT.	ESCUDIER.	SCHOTT.	MARTIN.	MEUMAN.

MANCHEGA.

ETUDE DE CONCERT

par

L. M. GOTTSCHALK.

(Seville 1853—1860.)

Ben Marcato e Staccato il Canto.

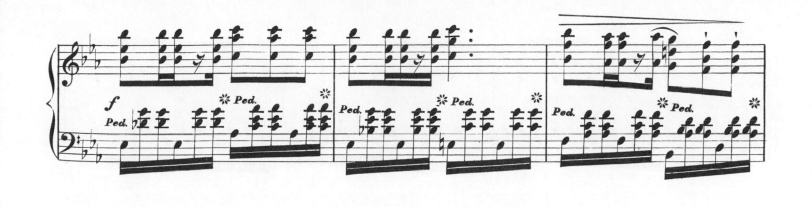

Ben marcato e staccato il canto.

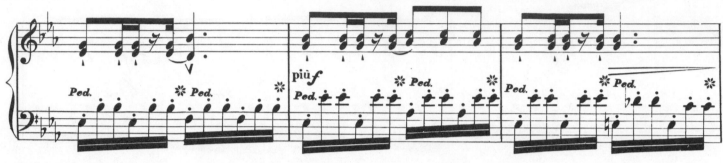

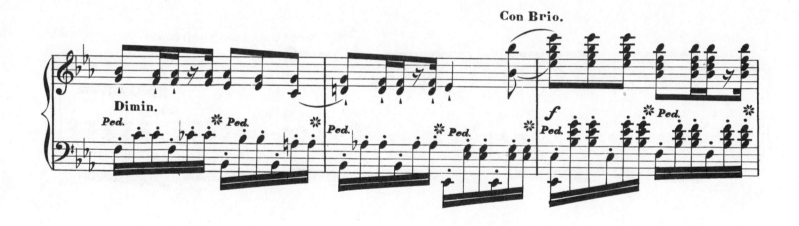

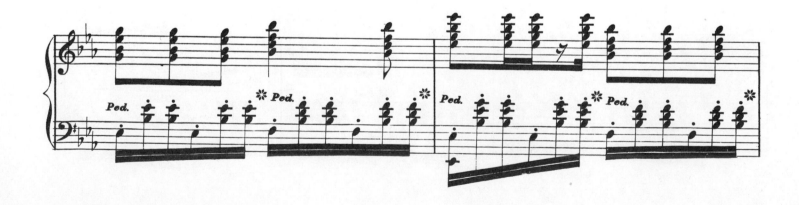

A MON CHER AMI NICHOLAS RUIZ Y ESPADERO DE LA HAVANE

MINUIT A SÉVILLE

Caprice

POUR

PIANO

PAR

L. M. Gottschalk

12½

NEW YORK
Published by William Hall & Son 543 Broadway.

Paris
LEON ESCUDIER

London
SCHOTT.

New Orleans
P. P. WERLEIN & CO.

MINUIT á SÉVILLE.

"En medio de mis pesares
Por vivir quise dormirme
Que el que vive como yo
Cuando duerme es cuando vive."

Tradicion andaluza.

L. M. Gottschalk.

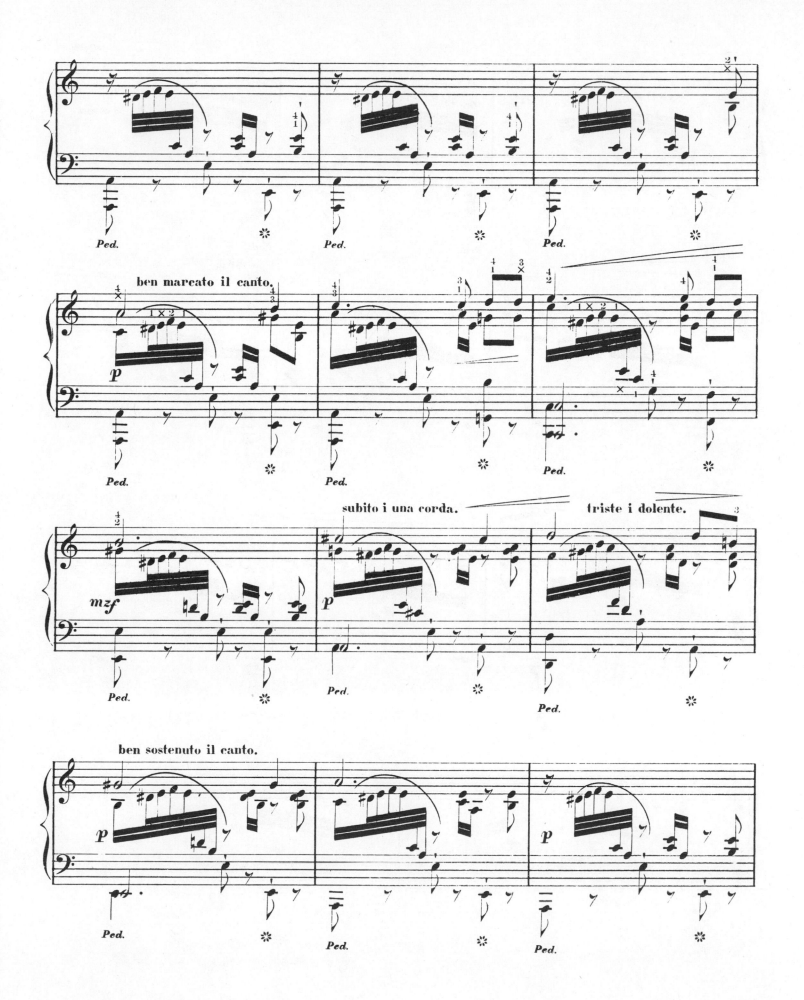

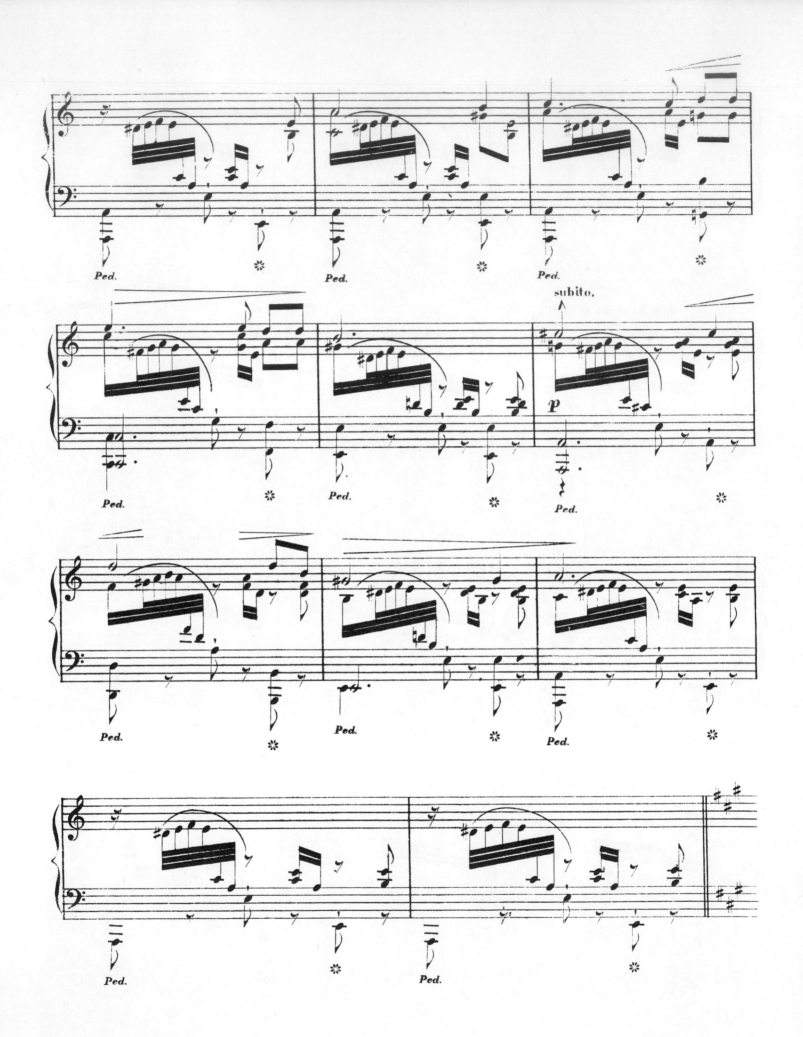

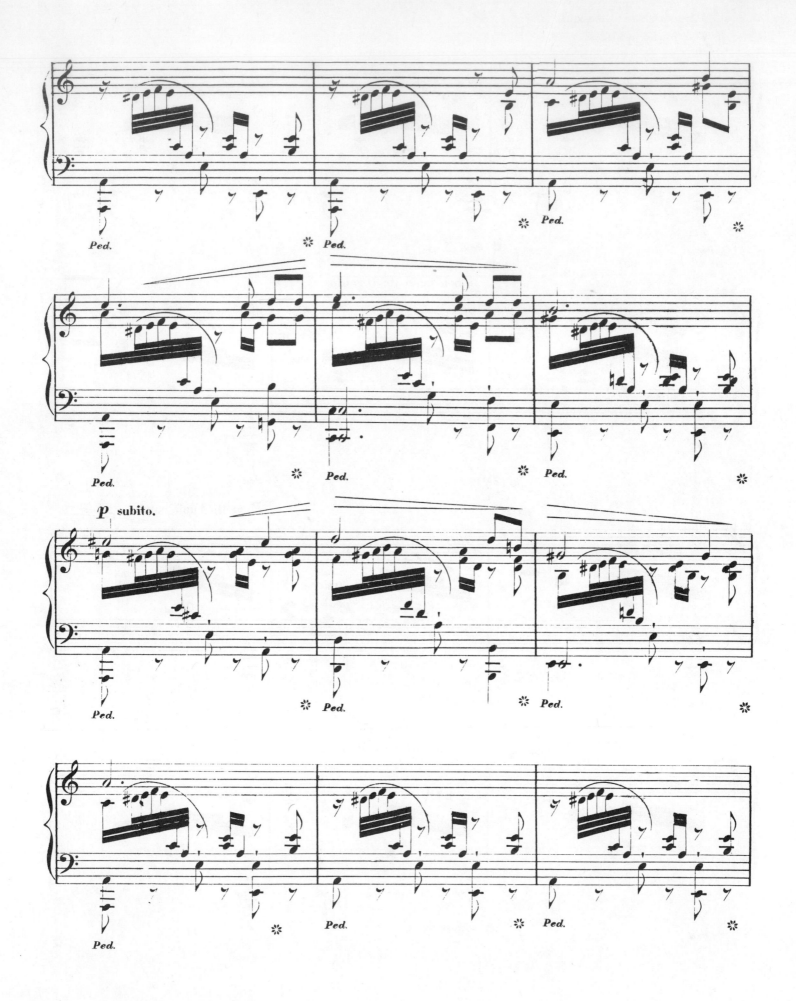

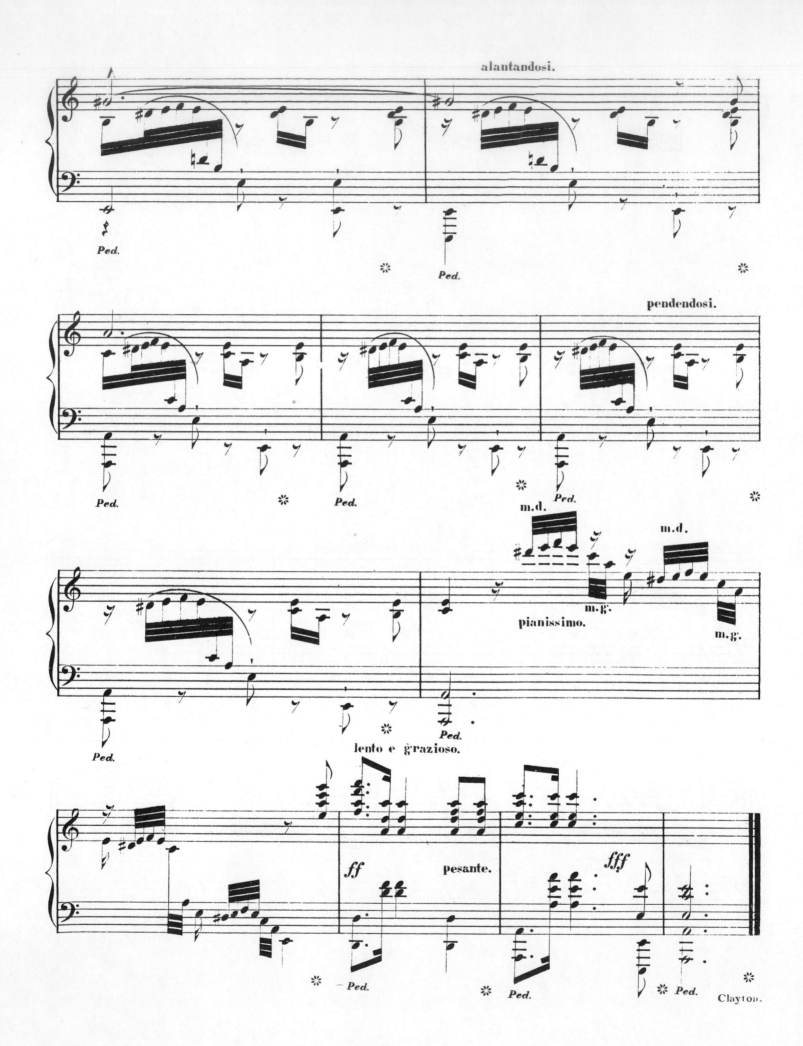

A MON AMI COLLIGNON.

SOUVENIRS D'ANDALOUSIE

CAPRICE DE CONCERT.

SUR LA CAÑA, LE FANDANGO, ET LE JALEO DE JEREZ.

COMPOSÉ PAR

L. M. GOTTSCHALK

STEVENS. SC.

10

*Le Cadre de ce morceau fut improvisé dans le Concert que donna
l'Auteur au Théâtre "del Circo" de Madrid le 16 Décembre 1851,
et fut ensuite exécuté tel qu'il est aujourd'hui à la "Soirée de Gala"
que donna S.A.R. le Duc de Montpensier au Palais de San Telmo
à Séville le 25 Aoüt 1852.*

New York

Published by William Hall & Son, 239 Broadway.

Entered according to Act of Congress AD 1855 by L.M.Gottschalk in the Clerk's Office of the District Court of the Eastern District of La

Paris, BUREAU CENTRAL.   Londres, SCHOTT.   Mayence, SCHOTT.   Milan, LUCCA.

SOUVENIRS D'ANDALOUSIE

CAPRICE DE CONCERT.

par

L. M. GOTTSCHALK.

according to Act of Congress in the year 1855 by L.M. GOTTSCHALK in the Clerks Office of the Dist:Court of the Eastern Dist: of L.ª

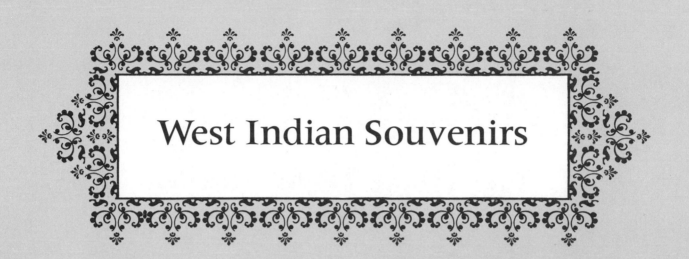

West Indian Souvenirs

A mon vieil ami

EDOUARD VERGER

(de Saint Pierre, Martinique.)

DANZA

pour

PIANO

Composée par

L. M. GOTTSCHALK

OP. 33.

Nº 15921.

Pr. 1Fl.

Propriété des Editeurs. Enregistré aux Archives de l'Union.

MAYENCE
chez les fils de B. Schott.

Bruxelles chez Schott frères.   Londres chez Schott & Cie
82 Montagne de la Cour.   159 Regent Street.

Dépôt général de notre fonds de Musique.

LEIPZIG   **ROTTERDAM**
C.F. Leede.   W.F. Lichtenauer.

Edition interdite en France et autorisée pour la Belgique.

PHILADELPHIA chez G. ANDRÉ & Cie

DANZA

par

L. M. GOTTSCHALK

Op: 33.

Porto - Rico Novembre 1857.

A mon vieil ami Edouard Verger
(de Saint Pierre, Martinique.)

Moderato quasi Andantino.

FINE.

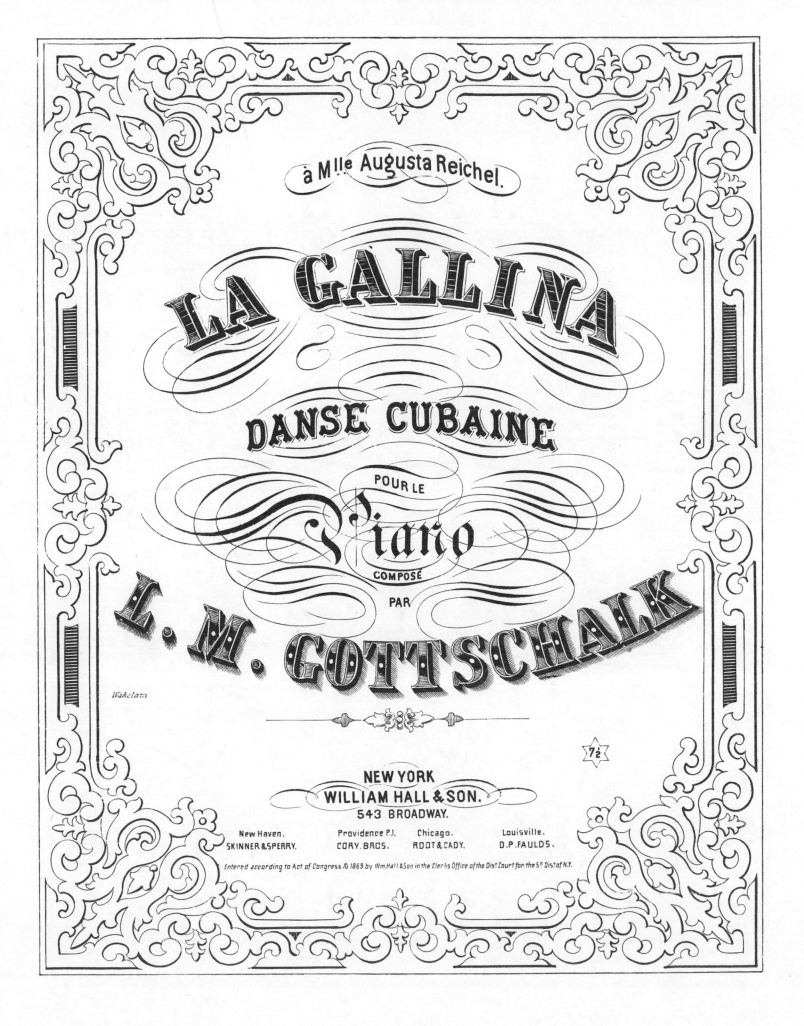

LA GALLINA.

(THE HEN)

DANSE CUBAINE.

L. M. GOTTSCHALK.

La Gallina (The Hen), Danse Cubaine 127

à Madame

Mennechet de Barival

LE MANCENILLIER

Sérénade

POUR LE

Piano

PAR

L.M. GOTTSCHALK.

Op. 11.

N° 11183

Pr.M

Propriété des Editeurs.

MAYENCE, B. SCHOTT'S SÖHNE.

Londres Schott & Cº.
159. Regent Street.

Bruxelles, Schott frères.
82. Montagne de la Cour.

Sydney, Schott & Cº
281. George Street.

LE MANCENILLIER.
SÉRÉNADE
par
L. M. GOTTSCHALK
(de la Louisiane)
Op: 11.

(1) **Passez au singe** $\not{\phi}$· **ad libitum.**

O, Ma charmante, epargnez moi!

(O my charmer, spare me)

CAPRICE

Par L. M. Gottschalk.

— 5 —

NEW YORK
Published by WILLIAM HALL & SON 543 Broadway.

Entered according to Act of Congress AD 1862 by William Hall & Son in the Clerks Office of the District Court of the Southern District of New York.

Note de l'Auteur

Je recommande pour ce petit morceau la plus scrupuleuse observation de ce qui est marqué. Le caractère d'ardeur à la fois mélancolique et inquiète que j'ai cherché à lui imprimer disparaîtrait entièrement, si l'exécutant ne s'attachait à donner aux rythmes qu'il renferme leur valeur exacte. La mélodie devra se détacher sur le fond tourmenté mais symetrique de la basse avec une sonorité "cantante" et une "morbidezza" qui sont les traits caractéristiques de la musique créole. Se mouvoir avec toute la désinvolture de = l'Ad Libitum = et du = tempo rubato = dans l'intérieur de la mesure, et ne point cependant en franchir les limites extrêmes, tel est le secret du charme que produit la musique des Antilles, et de la difficulté que présente ce morceau dont les mélodies et leur arrangement, bons ou mauvais, m'appartiennent entierement.

Note by the Author

I must suggest this little piece should be played exactly as it is written, as the license occasionally indulged in by pupils, of substituting their own thoughts for those of the composer, must inevitably interfere with the general effect. The characterestics of mingled sadness and restless passion which distinguish the piece would be utterly lost were not the accuracy of each changing rythm fully sustained. The melody should stand out in bold relief from the agitated but symetrical back-ground of the bass with the singing sonorousness and passionate languor which are the peculiar traits of Creole music. To give entire scope to the "Ad Libitum" and "Tempo Rubato" and at the same time not to transcend the extreme limits of the time, is the principal difficulty as well as the great charm of the music of the Antilles, from which I have borrowed the outline of this Composition, the Theme and Arrangement being exclusively my own. I intend hereafter, as a prelude to my pieces, to make a few observations on the proper method of playing them, hoping that those who like my music, may accept the fervent desire to facilitate its execution, as an acknowledgement of their kindly appreciation.

L.M.GOTTSCHALK.
New York 21 Juin 1862.

The Author in this morceau (which is entirely original) has endeavored to convey an idea of the singular rythm and charming character, of the music which exists among the Creoles of the Spanish Antilles. Chopin it is well known transfered the national traits of Poland, to his Mazurkas and Polonaises, and Mr. Gottschalk has endeavored to reproduce in works of an an appropriate chararacter, the characteristic traits of the Dances of the West Indias.

L. M. GOTTSCHALK.

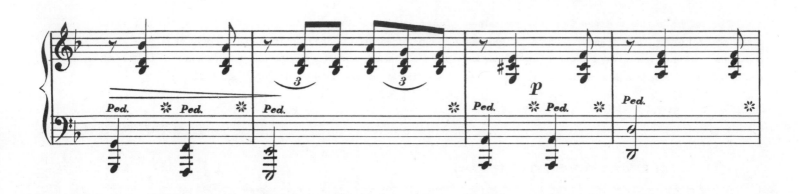

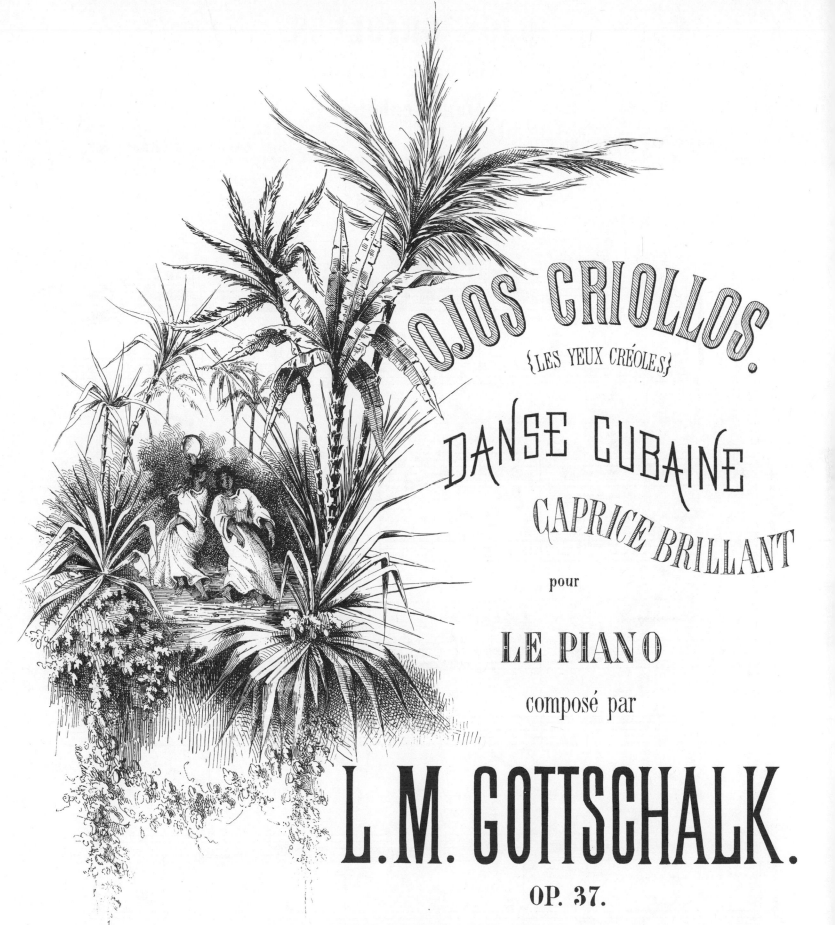

OJOS CRIOLLOS.

{LES YEUX CRÉOLES}

DANSE CUBAINE

CAPRICE BRILLANT

pour

LE PIANO

composé par

L. M. GOTTSCHALK.

OP. 37.

Proprieté des Editeurs Enregistré aux Archives de l'Union.

MAYENCE

chez les fils de B. Schott.

Bruxelles, Schott frères.   Londres Schott & Cⁱᵉ

82 Montagne de la Cour.   159 Regent Street.

Dépôt général de notre fonds de Musique :

LEIPZIG   **ROTTERDAM**

C.F. Leede.   W.F. Lichtenauer.

Edition interdite en France, et autorisée pour la Belgique.

16278.18008.

OJOS CRIOLLOS.

(LES YEUX CREOLES.)

Danse cubaine.

CAPRICE BRILLANT.

L. M. GOTTSCHALK Op. 37.

Fine.

À Mademoiselle
Maria Luisa del Rio Noguerido de Sedano
(de la Havane)

Souvenir

de la

HAVANE

Grande Caprice de Concert

Composée par

L. M. GOTTSCHALK.

Leeson

40

NEW YORK

Published by Wm HALL & SON 543 Broadway.

London.   Paris.   Mayence.   Madrid.   Lisbon.
SCHOTT.   ESCUDIER.   SCHOTT.   MARTIN.   MEUMAN.

SOUVENIR DE LA
HAVANE.

MODERATO. (♩ = 92.)

L. M. GOTTSCHALK.

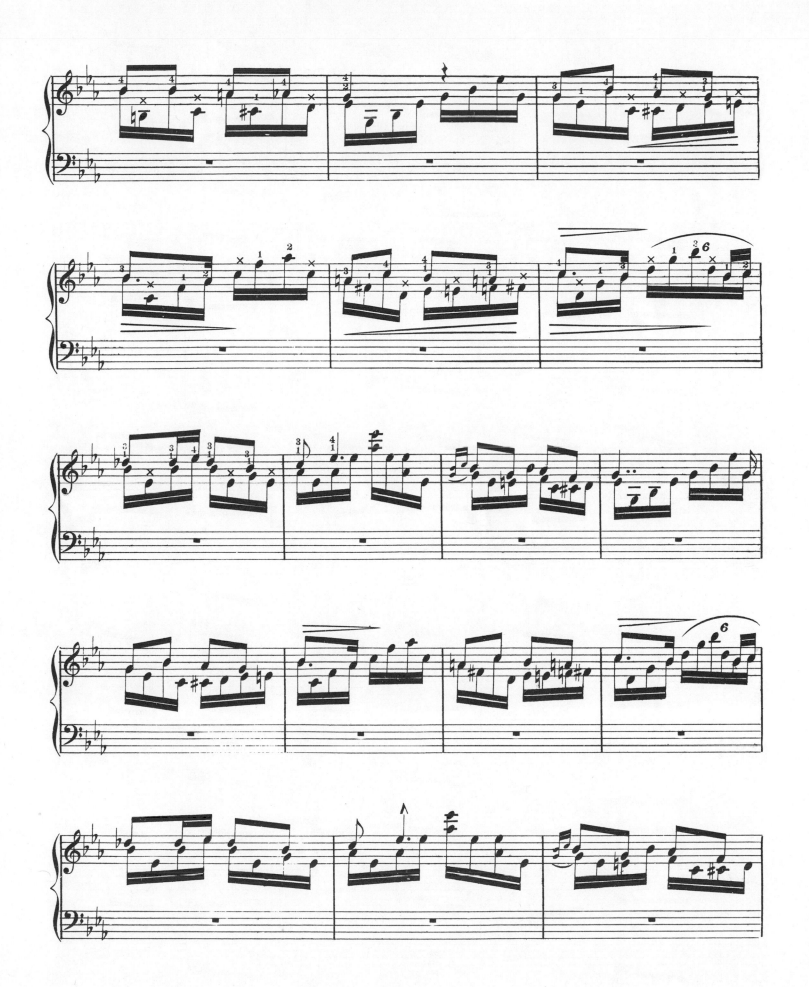

Souvenir de Porto Rico

Marche des Gibaros

pour

PIANO

par

L. M. GOTTSCHALK

OP. 31.

N° 15773.

Propriété des Editeurs

MAYENCE, B. SCHOTT'S SÖHNE

Londres, Schott & C°.
159 Regent Street

Bruxelles, Schott frères
82 Montagne de la Cour

P.

SOUVENIR DE PORTO RICO.

MARCHE DES GIBAROS

L. M. GOTTSCHALK Op. 31.

A MON AMI

Charles Fradel.

SUIS MOI!

CAPRICE

Composed by

L. M. GOTTSCHALK.

7½

NEW YORK

Published by Wm HALL & SON 543 Broadway.

Entered according to Act of Congress A.D 1862 by Wm. Hall & Son in the Clerks Office of the District Court of the Southern District of New York.

Note de l'Auteur

Je recommande pour ce petit morceau la plus scrupuleuse observation de ce qui est marqué. Le caractère d'ardeur à la fois mélancolique et inquiète que j'ai cherché à lui imprimer disparaîtrait entièrement, si l'exécutant ne s'attachait à donner aux rythmes qu'il renferme leur valeur exacte. La mélodie devra se détacher sur le fond tourmenté mais symetrique de la basse avec une sonorité "cantante" et une "morbidezza" qui sont les traits caractéristiques de la musique créole. Se mouvoir avec toute la désinvolture de = l'Ad Libitum = et du = tempo rubato = dans l'intérieur de la mesure, et ne point cependant en franchir les limites extrèmes, tel est le secret du charme que produit la musique des Antilles, et de la difficulté que présente ce morceau dont les mélodies et leur arrangement, bons ou mauvais, m'appartiennent entierement.

Note by the Author

I must suggest this little piece should be played exactly as it is written, as the license occasionally indulged in by pupils, of substituting their own thoughts for those of the composer, must inevitably interfere with the general effect. The characterestics of mingled sadness and restless passion which distinguish the piece would be utterly lost were not the accuracy of each changing rythm fully sustained. The melody should stand out in bold relief from the agitated but symetrical back-ground of the bass with the singing sonorousness and passionate languor which are the peculiar traits of Creole music. To give entire scope to the "Ad Libitum" and "Tempo Rubato" and at the same time not to transcend the extreme limits of the time, is the principal difficulty as well as the great charm of the music of the Antilles, from which I have borrowed the outline of this Composition, the Theme and Arrangement being exclusively my own. I intend hereafter, as a prelude to my pieces, to make a few observations on the proper method of playing them, hoping that those who like my music, may accept the fervent desire to facilitate its execution, as an acknowledgement of their kindly appreciation.

L.M. GOTTSCHALK.
New York 21 Juin 1862.

SUIS MOI!

CAPRICE.

The Author in this morceau (which is entirely original) has endeavored to convey an idea of the singular rythm and charming character, of the music which exists among the Creoles of the Spanish Antilles. Chopin it is well known transfered the national traits of Poland, to his Mazurkas and Polonaises, and Mr. Gottschalk has endeavored to reproduce in works of an appropriate character, the characteristic traits of the Dances of the West Indias.

L. M. GOTTSCHALK.

Concert and Salon Music
(Non-nationalistic)

6me Ballade

POUR

PIANO

PAR

L. M. Gottschalk

OP. 85.

Oeuvres posthumes publiés sur Manuscrits originaux avec autorisation de sa famille

PAR

N. R. ESPADERO.

Seule Edition legale et correcte.

N° 22255.

Pr. M. 1.75.

Propriété pour tous pays.

MAYENCE, B. SCHOTT'S SÖHNE.

Bruxelles Schott frères. Paris Editions Schott. Londres Schott & C°.
Montagne de la Cour.   Boul Malesherbes (40 Rue d'Anjou).   159 Regent Street.

6.ème BALLADE.

ŒUVRE POSTHUME.   **L.M.GOTTSCHALK** Op:85.

Stich und Druck von B.SCHOTT'S SÖHNE in Mainz.

Concert and Salon Music (Non-nationalistic)

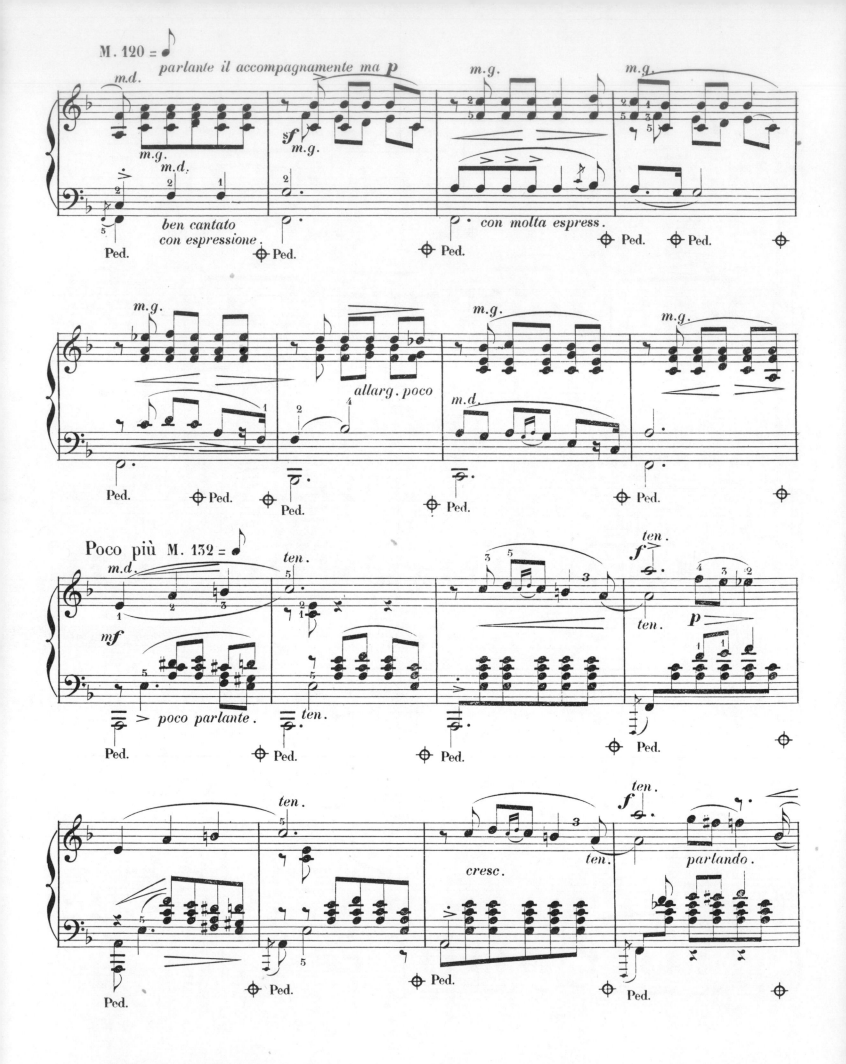

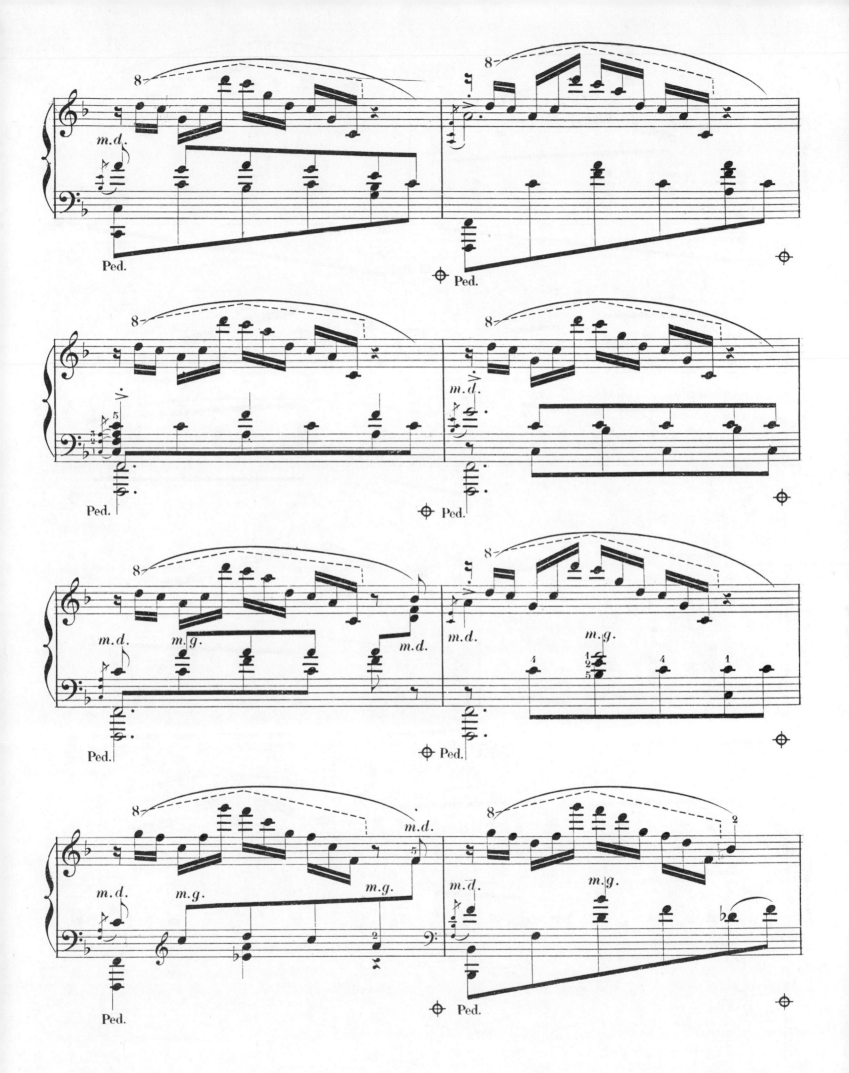

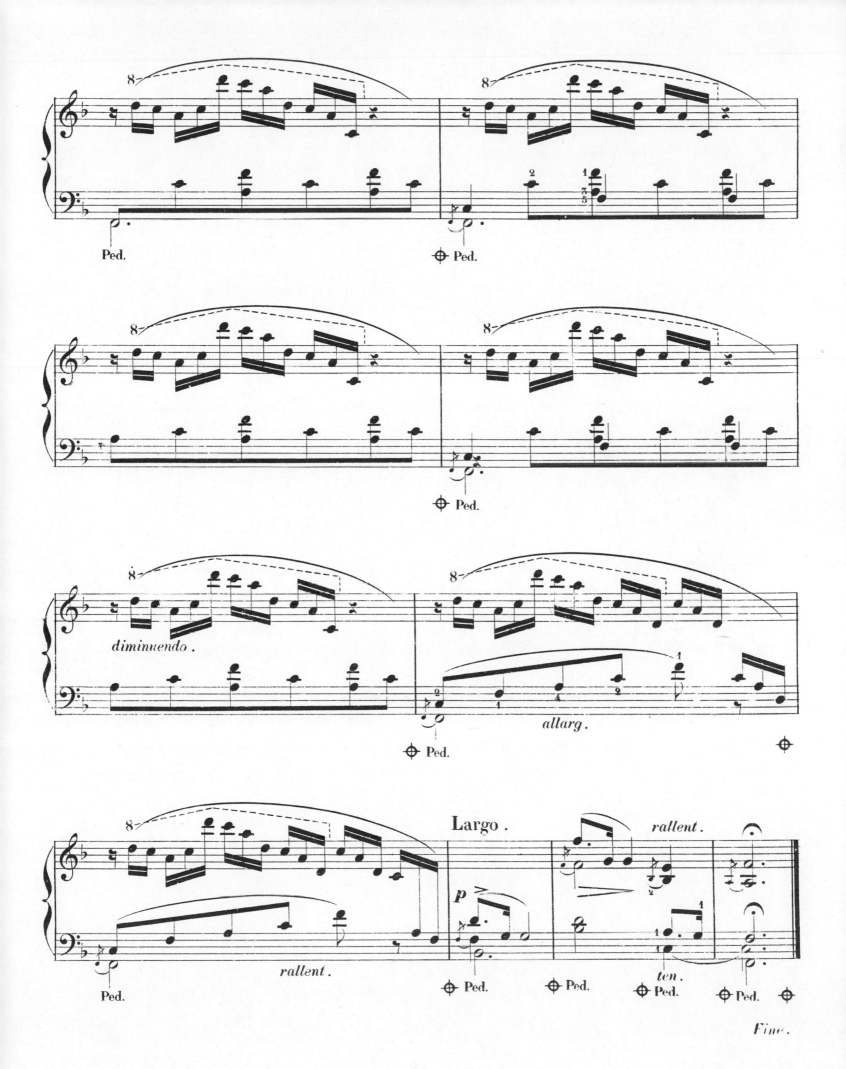

à Mlle Marie Damainville.

Berceuse
(Cradle Song)
Par
L. M. Gottschalk

10

NEW YORK
Published by WILLIAM HALL & SON 543 Broadway.

Entered according to Act of Congress AD 1862 by Wm. Hall & Son in the Clerks Office of the District Court of the South.º Dist. of N.York.

BERCEUSE.

(CRADLE SONG)

L. M. GOTTSCHALK.

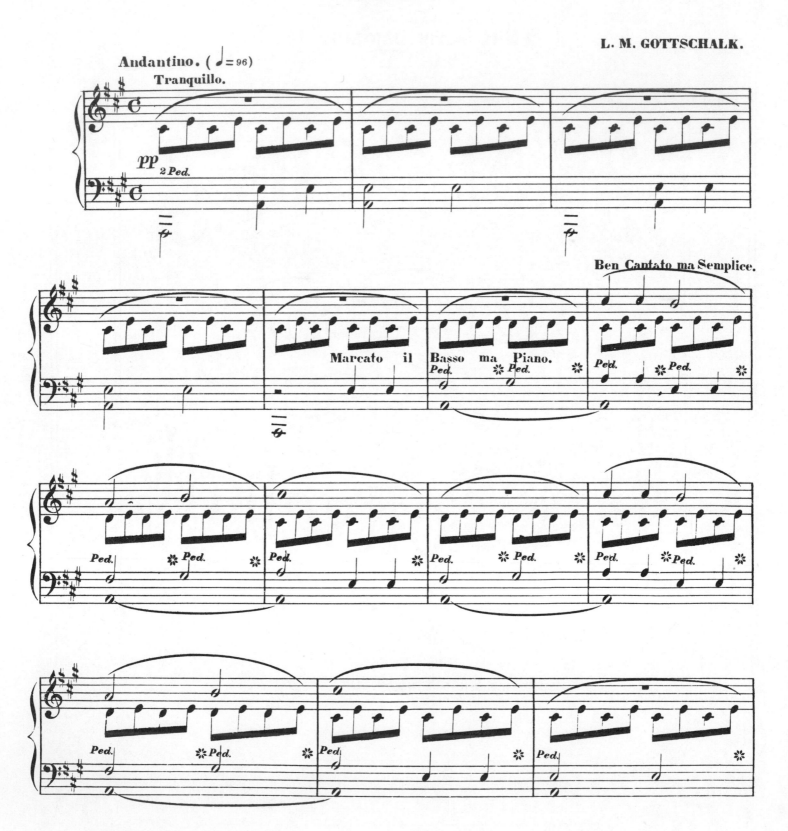

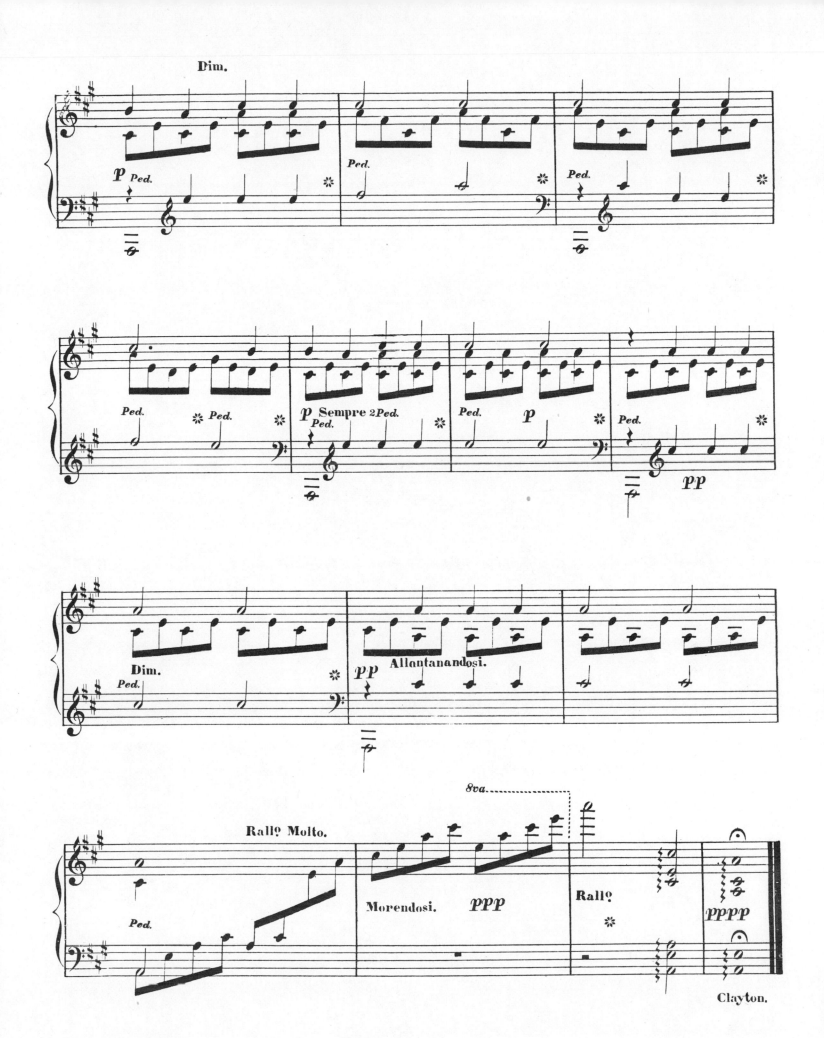

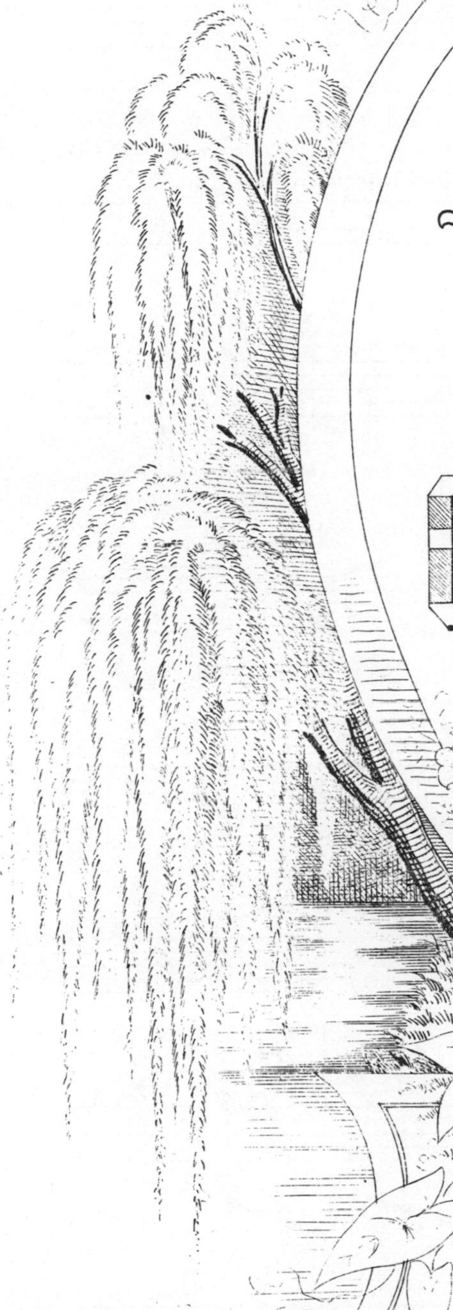

To

Mrs Geo. Henriques.

N. York.

THE DYING POET

Meditation.

Performed by

GOTTSCHALK

At his Concerts with immense success

Composed by

SEVEN OCTAVES.

6

BOSTON.

Published by Oliver Ditson & Co. 277 Washington St.

Cinn.	N. York	Boston.	Phil^a
J. Church Jr.	W. A. Pond & Co.	J. C. Haynes & Co.	J. E. Gould.

H. F. Greene, Eng.

THE DYING POET.

Comp. by S. OCTAVES.

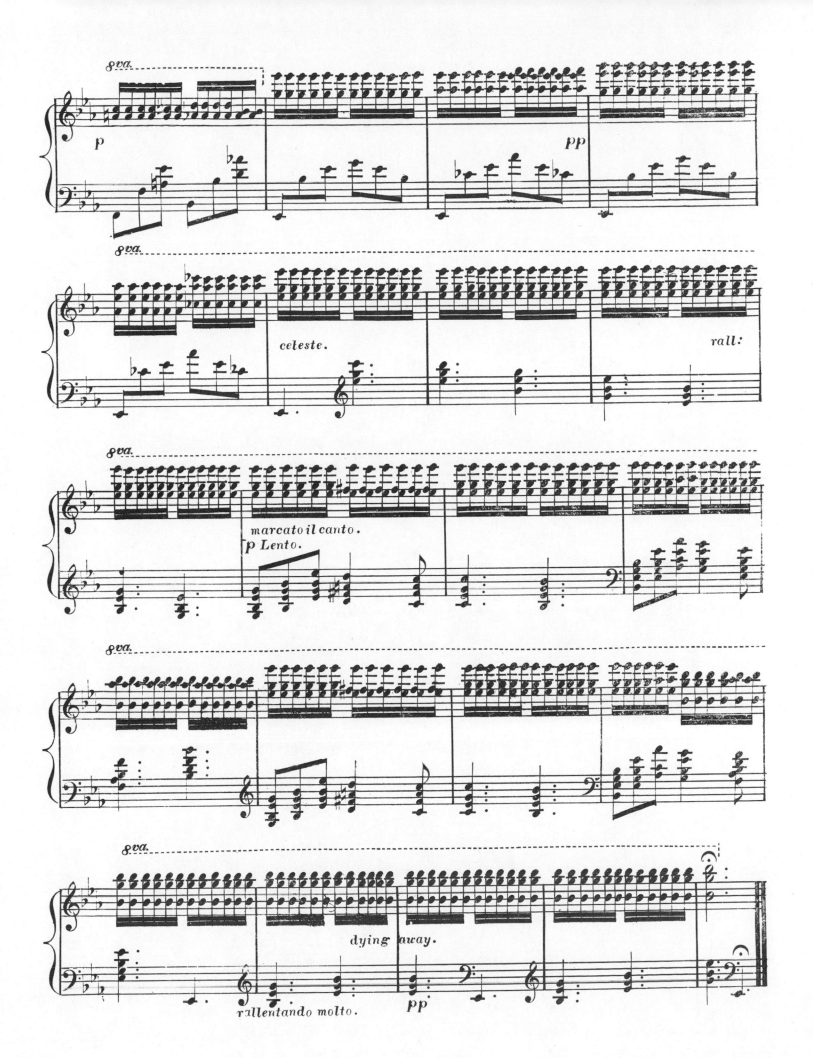

à mon ami

G. NESSLER.

Grand Scherzo

pour

PIANO

par

L. M. GOTTSCHALK.

OP. 57.

N° 20034.   Pr. .

Propriété des Editeurs.

MAYENCE, B. SCHOTT'S SÖHNE.

BRUXELLES, SCHOTT FRÈRES.   LONDRES, SCHOTT & C°
Montagne de la Cour.   159. Regent Street.

GRAND SCHERZO

L. M. GOTTSCHALK Op.57.

Stich u: Druck von B. SCHOTT'S SÖHNEN in Mainz.

Concert and Salon Music (Non-nationalistic)

Un poco meno mosso.

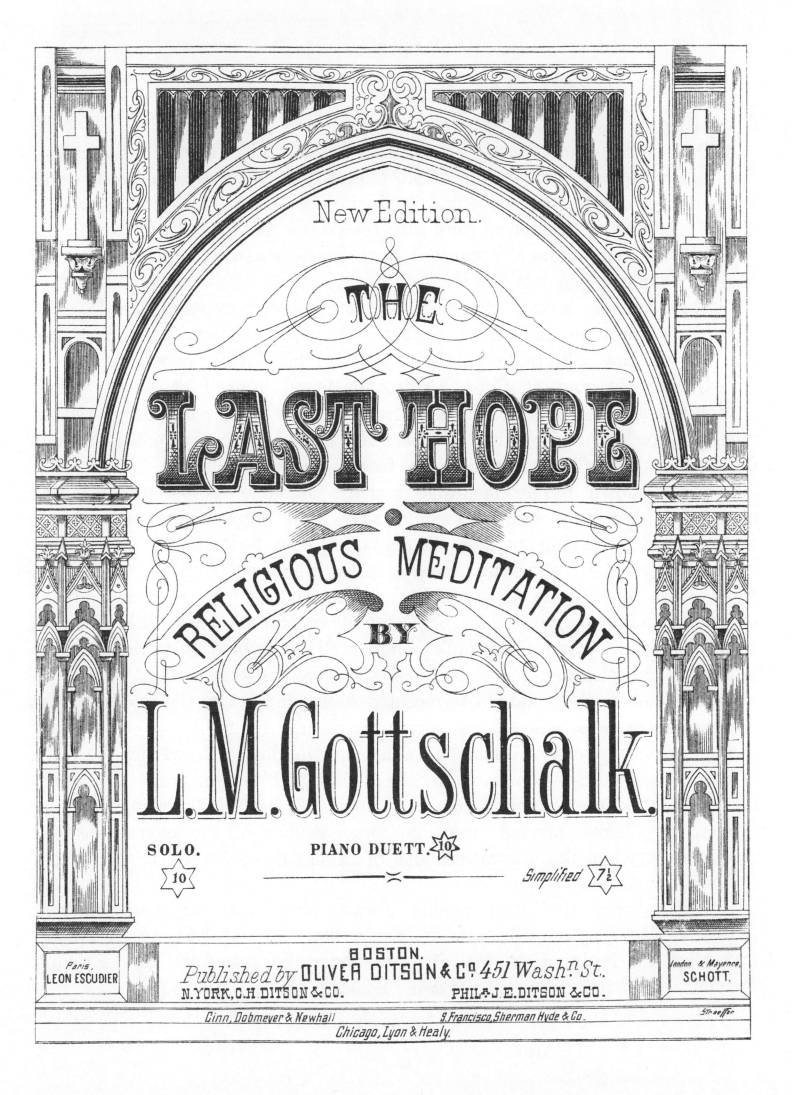

"THE LAST HOPE."

ONE of the most charming pianists of this city having observed— the ladies observe everything—that Gottschalk never passes an evening without executing, with profound religious sentiment, his poetic reverie "The Last Hope," asked of him his reason for so doing.

"It is," replied he, "because I have heart-memories, and that melody has become my evening prayer."

These words seemed to hide a mournful mystery, and the inquirer dared not question the artist further. A happy chance has given me the key to the admirable pianist's reply to his lovely questioner.

During his stay at Cuba, Gottschalk found himself at S——, where a woman of mind and heart, to whom he had been particularly recommended, conceived for him at once the most active sympathy, in one of those sweet affections almost as tender as maternal love.

Struck down by an incurable malady, Madame S—— mourned the absence of her only son, and could alone find forgetfulness of her sufferings while listening to her dear pianist, now become her guest and her most powerful physician. One evening, while suffering still more than usual—"In pity," said she, making use of one of the ravishing idioms of the Spanish tongue—"in pity, my dear Moreau, one little melody, the last hope!" And Gottschalk commenced to improvise an air at once plaintive and pleasing,—one of those spirit-breaths that mount sweetly to heaven, whence they have so recently descended. On the morrow, the traveller-artist was obliged to leave his friend, to fulfil an engagement in a neighboring city. When he returned, two days afterwards, the bells of the church of S—— were sounding a slow and solemn peal. A mournful presentiment suddenly froze the heart of Gottschalk, who, hurrying forward his horse, arrived upon the open square of the church just at the moment when the mortal remains of Senora S—— were brought from the sacred edifice.

This is why the great pianist always plays with so much emotion the piece that holy memories have caused him to name "The Last Hope," and why, in replying to his fair questioner, he called it his "Evening Prayer."—*Extract from "La France Musicale."*

GUSTAVE CHOUQUET.

New and only correct edition.
THE
LAST HOPE.

L.M. GOTTSCHALK.

Religioso.

The Last Hope, Religious Meditation   247

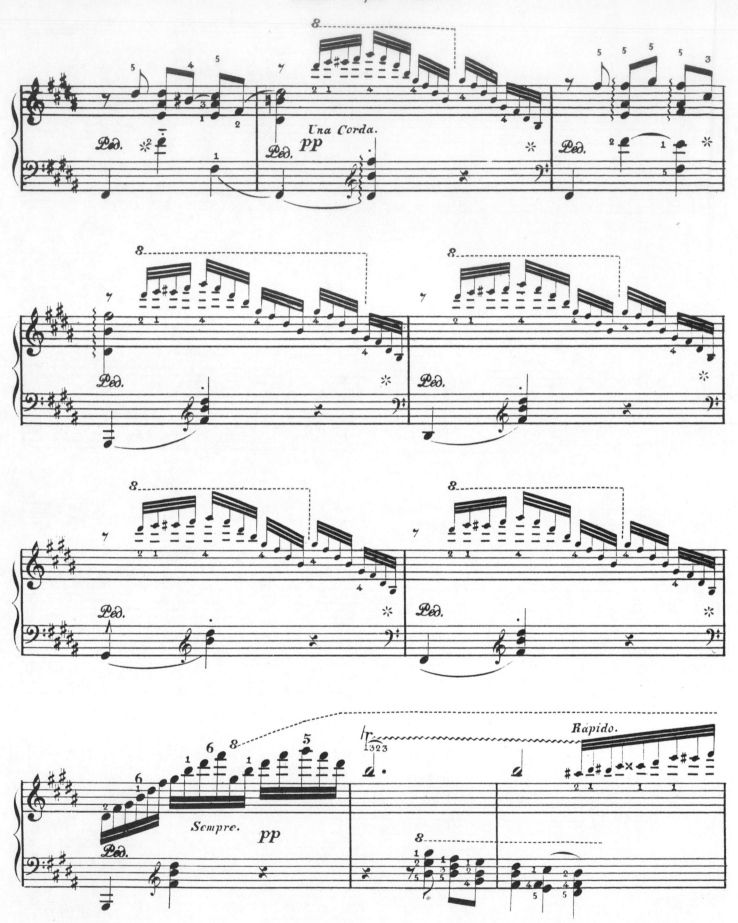

The Last Hope, Religious Meditation 255

MORTE!!

(SHE IS DEAD.)

LAMENTATION.

Par L. M. GOTTSCHALK.

Andante Moderato. (M.M. ♩=84.)

PIANO.

pp malinconico.

tranquillo.

Ent'd according to Act of Congress AD 1869 by Wm Hall & Son in the Clerk's Office of the Dis't Court of the Southern District of N.Y.

L. M. GOTTSCHALK'S
CHOICEST COMPOSITIONS

BANJO (GROTESQUE FANTASIE.)	1.25.	ORFA GRAND POLKA.	.75.
BERCEUSE (CRADLE SONG.)	.75.	OVERTURE TO Wm. TELL. *FOUR HANDS.*	2.50.
DYING POET.	75.	PASQUINADE.	.75.
HOME SWEET HOME.	1.00.	PRINTEMPS D'AMOUR MAZURKA.	1.50.
LAST HOPE. (RELIGIOUS MEDITATION.)	1.00.	RADIEUSE GRAND WALTZ. *SOLO 75. FOUR HANDS*	1.50.
MARCHE DE NUIT.	1.00.	RICORDATI. (NOCTURNE.)	.60.
MISERERE. (TROVATORE.)	1.25.	LA SCINTILLA. THE SPARK.	.75.
OJOS CRIOLLOS. (DANSE CUBAÏNE)	.75.	O LOVING HEART TRUST ON. *INE—INF—*	.60.
FOUR HANDS	1.25.	SLUMBER ON BABY DEAR. SONG.	.75.

BOSTON.
Published by OLIVER DITSON & CO. 451 Washington St.

NEW YORK.   SAVANNAH GA.   BALTIMORE MD.   CINCINNATI.   SAN FRANCISCO.   PHILA.
C. H. DITSON & CO.   LUDDEN & BATES.   OTTO SUTRO.   GEO. D. NEWHALL & CO.   SHERMAN CLAY & CO.   J. E. DITSON & CO.

CHICAGO.   St LOUIS.
LYON & HEALY.   J.H. Bufford's Sons Lith. Boston & New York.   J. L. PETERS.

PASQUINADE.

CAPRICE.

par L. M. GOTTSCHALK.

(M.M. ♩=84.)

Piano.

Concert and Salon Music (Non-nationalistic)

SES YEUX

POLKA DE CONCERT

POUR

PIANO

par

L. M. GOTTSCHALK

OP. 66.

Propriété des Editeurs

MAYENCE, B. SCHOTT'S SÖHNE.

BRUXELLES, SCHOTT FRÈRES.   LONDRES, SCHOTT & C°

Montagne de la Cour   159. Regent Street.

SES YEUX
POLKA DE CONCERT
POUR DEUX PIANOS
par L. M. GOTTSCHALK Op.66.

arr. par A. NAPOLEON.

Stich und Druck von B. SCHOTT'S SÖHNEN in Mainz.

(*) Pour jouer comme l'auteur, doublez le nombre de notes, jouant quatre percussions au lieu de deux, et changez les mains alternativement chaque quatre notes.

Concert and Salon Music (Non-nationalistic)

Concert and Salon Music (Non-nationalistic)

GOTTSCHALK'S Tournament GALOP.

Played by him at all his Concerts throughout the United States.

Pearson, Sc.

9

BOSTON
Published by OLIVER DITSON & Co 277 Washington St
H. WATERS. Agt. N.York.

TOURNAMENT GALOP.

L. M. GOTTSCHALK.

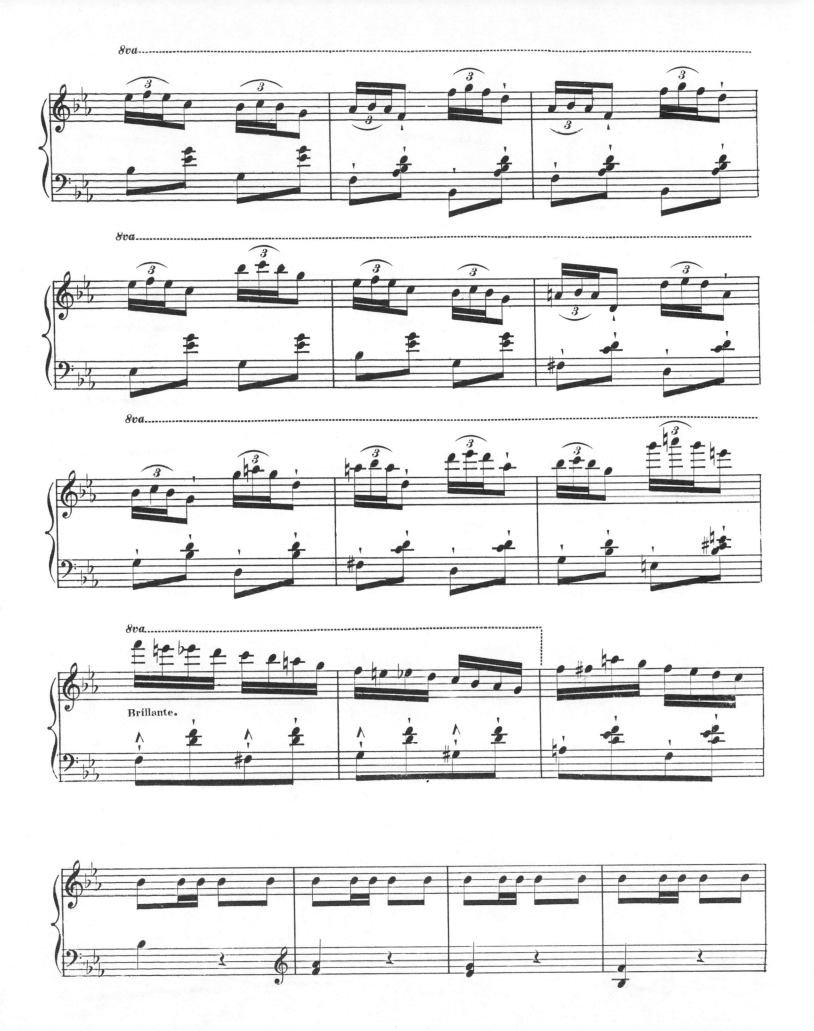

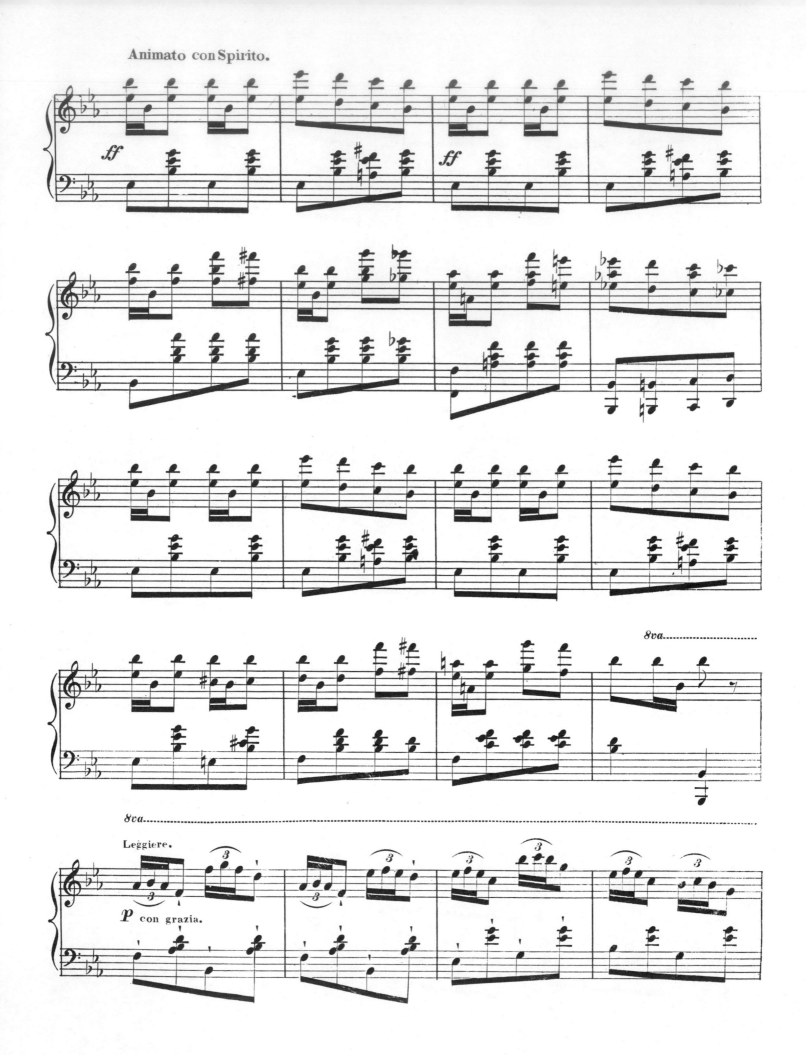